The International Finance Corporation

PRAEGER SPECIAL STUDIES IN
INTERNATIONAL ECONOMICS AND DEVELOPMENT

The International Finance Corporation

ORIGIN, OPERATIONS, AND EVALUATION

James C. Baker

FREDERICK A. PRAEGER, Publishers
New York • Washington • London

The purpose of the Praeger Special Studies is to make specialized research monographs in U.S. and international economics and politics available to the academic, business, and government communities. For further information, write to the Special Projects Division, Frederick A. Praeger, Publishers, 111 Fourth Avenue, New York, N.Y. 10003.

FREDERICK A. PRAEGER, PUBLISHERS
111 Fourth Avenue, New York, N.Y. 10003, U.S.A.
5, Cromwell Place, London S.W. 7, England

Published in the United States of America in 1968
by Frederick A. Praeger, Inc., Publishers

Library of Congress Catalog Card Number: 68-54999

Printed in the United States of America

TO
ALL THOSE DEDICATED
TO THE FIELD OF
DEVELOPMENT

PREFACE

The world has been moving gradually toward two diverse economically developed camps which U Thant has called the war between North and South. Twenty years of foreign economic assistance of the under-developed areas by the industrialized nations have witnessed a variety of international and national development financing institutions and methods for dispensing this aid. Emphasis on one type of institution or method is constantly changing. The trend of foreign economic assistance has changed from reconstruction of war-torn countries to development of low-income nations. The direction of aid has been shifting from complete emphasis on public social overhead capital projects to more financing of private industrial projects. Industrial emphasis has shifted from basic sectors such as steel, cement, and other heavy manufacturing industries to more attention toward such industries as agribusiness. Thus, new patterns of world economic assistance have been slowly emerging in recent years.

One very successful international development financing institution is the International Finance Corporation (IFC), a part of the World Bank Group, in operation since 1956. IFC is the only world-wide international financial institution which finances private enterprise projects in member countries without government guarantee. In addition, IFC also is empowered to take an equity position in companies which it finances. Thus, this financial institution is well equipped to facilitate the new patterns in world economic assistance because of its complete emphasis on private enterprise and its ability to invest in sectors such as agribusiness.

During the past several years, a number of books have been written about, or which analyzed in part, the World Bank Group, the World Bank itself, and the International Development Association (IDA),

the youngest of the World Bank Group agencies.
Among these are The Road to Huddersfield: A Journey
to Five Continents by James Morris (New York: Pan-
theon Books, 1963), a biography of the World Bank;
and The International Development Association: A
New Approach to Foreign Aid by James H. Weaver (New
York: Frederick A. Praeger, 1965). Other books,
monographs, and pamphlets about various aspects of
these institutions have been published by the World
Bank Group itself. However, no book describing and
analyzing the operations of the International Finance Corporation has been published outside the
World Bank Group. Only B.E. Matecki's Establishment
of the International Finance Corporation and United
States Policy (New York: Frederick A. Praeger, 1957)
has covered IFC and this was a study only of the
origin of IFC. Thus, as successful as IFC has been
since 1956 in fulfilling a very unique developmental
role, the lack of an analysis and evaluation of the
first decade of its operations seemed significant
and a desire to remedy this inadequacy in the literature of development finance began to develop over
two years ago. This study is the culmination of
that desire.

The Washington, D.C., area offered a wealth of
research assistance for such a subject. It is the
situs of the World Bank Group headquarters including
IFC and IDA. The State Department, with its country desk officers and Agency for International Development, and the numerous embassies of IFC member
countries were valuable as sources of interviews
with officials highly knowledgeable of IFC's
activities.

In addition to these research facilities,
press releases, annual reports, and other special
reports released by the World Bank and IFC were
highly valuable sources of information. Additional
insight into individual cases of IFC activities was
furnished by IFC-financed companies themselves.
Many such companies forwarded annual reports,
letters, and other data about their operations.
Finally, government publications such as congres-

sional hearings and committee study reports were
utilized in analyzing the origin of IFC.

This study is organized so that the origin,
general and specific operations, problems, and
value can be studied within the framework of the
dynamism of today's changing patterns in world
economic assistance. Chapter 1 covers the history
and framework of aid including discussion of these
new patterns. IFC emerges in Chapter 2 as a very
important institution with regard to these new
patterns. The background of the origin of IFC is
presented in this chapter. Objectives, administration, and specific operational methods are described in Chapters 3 and 4.

Specific case studies of companies financed
by IFC are presented in Chapters 5 through 8. Fifteen companies have been selected for a number of
reasons. A variety of industries are represented
and both highly successful and struggling companies
are included. These companies are located in all
major geographical areas. In addition to these fifteen selected cases, all development finance company
investments made by IFC in the four areas are described in these four chapters.

The next two chapters offer an analysis of the
problems incurred in IFC's development financing as
well as a summary and evaluation of the first decade
of IFC's operations. Finally, in Chapter 11, an
attempt is made to predict the future of the International Finance Corporation. Suggestions are made
as to what new investment interests IFC might cul-
tivate.

Some final comments about acknowledgments are
in order. The idea of a study of the International
Finance Corporation germinated in graduate school
at Indiana University in my coursework in international business administration and economic development. Two professors must be singled out for their
assistance in the development of this idea. Professor Stefan J. Robock, now at Columbia University,

encouraged the development of my interest in both areas mentioned, and Professor Louis Shere, a fiscal expert in the Economics Department at Indiana, developed a seminar in financial problems of less developed countries in which the World Bank Group was thoroughly analyzed.

The staff of the International Finance Corporation was extremely helpful. Space does not permit listing all who assisted this project but a few must be mentioned. The Director of Information, Frank O'Brien, and his assistants, Donald Roessner and Julian Grenfel, not only granted me their valuable time but also furnished me with information as well as appointments with IFC officials. William Diamond, Director of IFC's Development Finance Companies Department, and various investment officers in the organization read my manuscript and contributed many helpful suggestions for improvement. I am deeply grateful for the assistance rendered by these IFC officials.

I wish to express my thanks to all other interviewees mentioned in the study and those who wished to remain anonymous. Their valuable insights as officials of the U.S. State Department, foreign embassies and private and public institutions were extremely valuable in developing the analysis of IFC's operations. Although those mentioned specifically and anonymously here assisted me in ways too numerous to mention, I must accept all responsibility for any errors or shortcomings in this study.

Finally, I must acknowledge the assistance of my wife, Jean. Her patience and understanding in assisting me with the preparation of the manuscript in its many stages are comparable to an investment commitment by IFC to an industrial project. Without the IFC commitment, the project would fail. Without my wife's encouragement--in many ways--and assistance, this project would have failed.

Beltsville, Maryland   J.C.B.

CONTENTS

LIST OF TABLES

ABBREVIATIONS

AID	Agency for International Development
AKU	Algemene Kunstzijde
BANDESCO	Banco del Desarrollo Economico Español, S.A.
BIDI	Banque Ivoirienne de Développement Industriel, S.A.
BNDE	Banque Nationale pour le Développement Economique of Morocco
CAVENDES	C.A. Venezolana de Desarrollo
CDC	Colonial Development Corporation
CVF	Corporación Venezolana de Fomento
DFC	Development finance company
ECOSOC	Economic and Social Council
FEMSA	Fábrica Español Magnetos, S.A.
FERTISA	Fertilizantes Sinteticos, S.A.
IBRD	International Bank for Reconstruction and Development
IDA	International Development Association
IDB	Industrial Development Bank (Turkey)
IDB	Inter-American Development Bank
IFC	International Finance Corporation

IFCI	Industrial Finance Corporation of India
IFCT	Industrial Finance Corporation of Thailand
IFF	Industrialization Fund of Finland
IMF	International Monetary Fund
LBIDI	Liberian Bank for Industrial Development and Investment
LDC	Less developed country
MIDFL	Malaysian Industrial Development Finance Ltd.
MUSCO	Mahindra-Ugine Steel Company
NIBID	National Investment Bank for Industrial Development, S.A.
NIDB	Nigerian Industrial Development Bank, Ltd.
NOFC	Netherlands Overseas Finance Company
OECD	Organization for Economic Cooperation and Development
PASA	Petroquimica Argentina, S.A.I.C.
PDCP	Private Development Corporation of the Philippines
PICIC	Pakistan Industrial Credit and Investment Corporation, Ltd.
SNI	Société Nationale d'Investissement
SOFINA	Société Financière de Transports et d'Entreprises Industrielles, S.A.

SUNFED   Special United Nations Fund for
                 Economic Development

TAMSA   Tubos de Acero de Mexico, S.A.

VKCM   Vereenigde Klattensche Cultuur
                 Maatschappij

YPF   Yacimientos Petroliferos Fiscales

The International Finance Corporation

CHAPTER **1** NEW PATTERNS OF
WORLD ASSISTANCE
IN ECONOMIC
DEVELOPMENT

THE CHALLENGE

U Thant, Secretary-General of the United
Nations, once told members attending the Fifth
World Conference of the Society for International
Development that the relevant war was not between
East and West, but between North and South.[1] He
was referring to the industrialized nations, located principally in the northern hemisphere and
the less-developed countries, located mainly in
the southern hemisphere. Robert Heilbroner refers
to a hundred or more nations which may be classified as being within the category of "less-
developed countries" because of relatively low
incomes per capita.[2] In a United Nations document
outlining proposals for a "Development Decade" in
the 1960's, it is pointed out that higher standards
of living are suppressed because of the "higher
rates of population growth in developing countries
than in wealthier countries."[3] Paul Hoffmann
writes of these problems as well as the disease,
illiteracy, poverty, and hunger of two thirds of
the world's 3 billion inhabitants.[4] Hoffmann,
director of the U.N. Development Program, and
before that director of the U.N. Special Fund, and
principal designer of the United States Marshall
Plan program of aid for postwar reconstruction of
Europe, describes the awakening of the industrialized nations in becoming aware of, and attempting

to alleviate, the problems of the developing nations.[5]   Irving S. Friedman, Economic Adviser to
the President of the International Bank for Reconstruction and Development--the World Bank, in an
address to the Canadian Political Science Association, calls this process, whereby the rich nations
are assisting the development of these countries:
a "profound new development...in human affairs
[which] may well be the most distinguishing feature
of our age."[6]

It is this challenge of fulfilling the needs
of the low-income nations which led to many proposals and studies concerning world aid in the late
1950's and early 1960's. This challenge led to the
proposal for a United Nations Development Decade in
which incomes of the less-developed countries (LDC's)
would be increasing by 5 per cent per annum by 1970
and that measures would be established to maintain
this growth rate thereafter. The program required
population growth rates of no more than 2 to 2.5
per cent per annum so that per capita incomes in
the LDC's could double within twenty-five to thirty
years.[7] Heilbroner stated the following as terms
of this challenge which he called "the Great Ascent":

1.   Economic development is not primarily an
economic but a political and social process;

2.   The political and social changes required
for economic development are apt to be
revolutionary in nature;

3.   Economic development is not a process
which breeds social contentment;

4.   The Great Ascent is not assured of success;

5.   The price of development is apt to be
political and economic authoritarianism.[8]

Finally, Robert Theobald couches this challenge in
much less subtle terms when he states the stability
and existence of the LDC's necessitates rapid development which will occur only if the industrialized
nations give aid to the LDC's.[9]

INTERNATIONAL AID

Introduction

Although international trade and investment
are business functions which are centuries old,
the practice of deliberate assistance of low income
countries by industrialized nations is a relatively
new concept. This practice has accelerated since
World War II and the internationalization of aid
began in earnest with the Bretton Woods Agreement
of 1944 from which evolved the International Bank
for Reconstruction and Development (IBRD) and the
International Monetary Fund. The IBRD, or World
Bank, performed as its first principal activity
assistance in the reconstruction of war-torn
nations. In addition, the United Nations and its
agencies were established in 1945. These were the
first concrete efforts in international aid involving multilateral agencies.

During the late-1940's, the United States
initiated the Marshall Plan for channeling aid bilaterally to Western Europe for reconstruction
purposes. U.S. aid was also given at this time to
Greece and Turkey in their struggles against Com-
munism and revolution. In 1947, the U.S. State
Department created a Coordinator for Aid to Greece
and Turkey, and Congress appropriated $400 million
for such aid under the Truman Doctrine.[10] In 1948,
the Foreign Assistance Act was passed by the U.S.
Congress establishing an Economic Cooperation
Administration and appropriating $6 billion for
reconstruction of Western Europe. This was the
Marshall Plan and it established the American
foreign aid program.[11]

Multilateral Aid

The principal multilateral financial institutions will be briefly described in this section.
These are institutions which are comprised of large

international governmental memberships, which dispense financial aid--as opposed to the Colombo Plan
which dispenses only technical and managerial advice and equipment or other materials--and which do
not impose political sanctions or other requirements
on aid recipients.

International Bank for Reconstruction and Development (IBRD)

The IBRD was established in 1944, had 106
members as of July, 1967, and has a contributed
capitalization of over $20 billion. IBRD grants
loans with maturities of, generally, 15 years and
interest rates of 5.5 to 6 per cent. Its funds
are obtained from the usable portion of members'
contributions, its own borrowings, earnings, sales
of portions of its loans, and repayments. The
World Bank, as of July, 1967, had made loans
totaling $10,670 million in 82 countries. These
loans are government-guaranteed and are principally
for social infrastructure projects initiated by
member governments. During the period 1963-1967,
the World Bank's loans averaged $800 to 1,000 mil-
lion annually.[12]

International Development Association (IDA)

IDA was formed as part of the World Bank Group
in 1960 as a means of lending capital, with very
soft terms, to LDC's. The loans are to IBRD member
countries, must be government-guaranteed and for
social infrastructure projects with the same high
financial and technical standards as World Bank-
financed projects, but the terms are fifty-year
maturities with ten-year grace periods and they
require no interest payments. Only a small administrative fee is levied. As of June 30, 1967, IDA
had granted $1.78 billion to its poorer member
countries. More than 70 per cent of this has gone
to India and Pakistan. IDA is financed by members'
contributions and subscriptions.[13] However, IDA
will not allow member countries which contribute to
attach conditions specifying how much of the contribution should be spent in the donor country.

International Finance Corporation (IFC)

The IFC is the subject of this study, thus the
only statement to be made at this time is that it
is the only fully international institution which
gives assistance to the private enterprise sector
without government guarantee. IFC was established
in 1956 and is part of the World Bank Group. As of
June 30, 1967, IFC had committed funds totaling
$221 million in 36 countries.[14] However, because
this aid is very catalytic in nature, more explana-
tion is necessary in later chapters.

Regional Development Banks

A number of regional development banks have
been formed. The oldest of these is the Inter-
American Development Bank (IDB), established in
1959. In recent years, the African and Asian
Development Banks have been created but insufficient time has passed for their activities to be
adequately assessed. In testimony by U.S. Secretary
of State Dean Rusk before the U.S. Senate Foreign
Relations Committee on March 11, 1968, Secretary
Rusk stated that the African Development Bank had
just made its first loan and that the U.S. Congress
was being asked to appropriate $400 million for the
Asian Development Bank.

The IDB's membership consists of the Latin
American countries and the United States. Total
capitalization is nearly 1 billion dollars. Loans
are made on somewhat the same terms as those made
by the World Bank and for much the same type
projects.

Summary

These agencies all exist to foster economic
development of member countries and all except IFC
operate on strictly a loan basis with only IDA
granting soft loans. All told these institutions
have over $25 billion of capitalization and have
contributed over $13 billion to economic assistance
of the LDC's. Other agencies such as the U.N.

Special Fund (which specialized in preinvestment
studies), other U.N. agencies, the Colombo Plan,
and the institutions of the European Economic Community also dispense aid on a multilateral basis.

Bilateral Aid

The United States

Bilateral aid from the United States is administered principally by the Agency for International
Development (AID) which is the most recent of a
number of U.S. agencies designed for this purpose.
Congress appropriates funds by the Foreign Assistance Act and these are channeled to LDC's through
AID. The Food for Peace Program under P.L. 480
disposes of U.S. agricultural surpluses and some
assistance on a long-term loan basis is administered by the U.S. Export-Import Bank. U.S. aid
through these programs is the most important element of international aid given bilaterally.[15]

U.S. economic aid substantially increased
annually from about $2 billion in 1956 to $3.7
billion in 1963.[16] However, since 1963, U.S.
foreign aid appropriations have been reduced by
Congress each year. President Johnson's request
for FY 1968 of $3.1 billion was the lowest request
in U.S. history[17] and the $2.3 billion appropriated
was also the lowest U.S. appropriation in history.[18]

The declining trend of U.S. bilateral aid
began in 1963 when more emphasis was put on solving
the persistent deficit problem of the U.S. balance
of payments. The Clay Committee Report of 1963,
chaired by General Lucius Clay and commissioned by
President John Kennedy, placed emphasis on a shift
in three principal areas of U.S. aid:

1. provide more economic aid for long-term
development and less for current budget
support;

2.   emphasize the transition of developing
countries to self-support wherever possible;

3.   increase reliance on private enterprise
for development, and extend the use of private
resources in the AID program.[19]

Since the Clay Committee Report, U.S. aid disbursements have not only decreased in amount, they
have been concentrated on a smaller number of nations which are becoming better able to support
themselves. For instance, the country programs
proposed by the FY 1968 U.S. AID Foreign Aid Program show that 87 per cent of AID's funds for
country programs will go to sixteen countries; 82
per cent of AID's development loans will go to only
eight countries; 90 per cent of AID's supporting
assistance will go to only four nations: Vietnam,
Korea, Laos, and Thailand.[20] AID emphasizes its
belief that the private sector is the key to success in the developing countries.[21]

The U.S. AID disbursement for FY 1967 was
about $2.4 billion for economic assistance and
nearly another billion for military assistance.[22]
Since 1956, the high mark for U.S. official net
flow of financial resources to LDC's was the $3.7
billion of 1963.[23]

Other Industrialized Nations

The bilateral aid to LDC's by nations other
than the United States is disbursed principally by
the member nations of the Organization for Economic
Cooperation and Development (OECD) including the
Western European nations, Canada, and Japan. A
number of the European nations maintain bilateral
aid ties with former colonies, e.g., Belgium,
France, and Great Britain with former African
colonies.

Since 1961, aid from the OECD nations has been
declining, relatively speaking. In 1961, these
nations dispensed over $2.7 billion in official
financial transfers to the LDC's. Thus, with the

nearly $3.5 billion of official U.S. aid, the total
OECD aid appropriation for 1961 was $6.134 billion.[24]
Coupled with the 1961 OECD net private long-term
investments and guaranteed private export credits
to LDC's, the total flow of financial resources to
LDC's in 1961 was $9.22 billion.[25]

However, official outlays from the industrialized nations, slightly over $6 million in 1961, are
still running at about $6 billion annually in 1967-
68. During this six- to seven-year period, the
output of the industrialized nations has increased
by about $200 billion. None of this increase in
the GNP of the OECD countries has been reflected in
official aid appropriations to the LDC's during
this period.[26]

David Rockefeller states that the total gross
national product of the world's industrial nations
is about $1.5 trillion annually. One of the U.N.
Development Decade's recommendations called for
assistance from these nations to the LDC's approxi-
mating 1 per cent of their combined outputs.[27]
Rockefeller also recommends the 1 per cent figure
and that such appropriations would result in aid
flows to the LDC's of $15 billion annually. How-
ever, he believes more international assistance
must be in the form of multilateral aid for this
amount to be reached.[28] At any rate, the present
flow of international aid amounts to only 40 per
cent of the amount recommended by Rockefeller and
the United Nations.

Officials of the World Bank have given a
number of reasons for the trend to relatively de-
creasing aid flows from industrialized nations to
LDC's. Among these are: 1) the LDC's lack the
capacity to absorb more debt on conventional terms;
2) the general shortage of world capital drives up
interest rates and makes investment in developed
nations more attractive; and 3) the political instability in most of the LDC's has caused possible
investors in developed countries to become dis-
illusioned about the profit potential of the LDC's.[29]

Other reasons have been presented for the declining flows of official aid to LDC's. John Adler
of the World Bank believes the poor performance by
industrialized nations is because foreign aid was
proposed on erroneous grounds that "one big push
with lots of aid will cause a once-and-for-all
transformation." He believes there is need to con-
vince lawmakers that foreign aid is a never-ending,
long-term process.[30] Max Millikan, Director of the
Center for International Studies, Massachusetts
Institute of Technology, believes that the tight-
ening U.S. economy, the decline in the Cold War,
and the Vietnamese War, are the principal reasons
for declining American aid appropriations.[31]

The International Development Association was
formed to alleviate part of these problems, namely
the inability of many LDC's to absorb debt on conventional terms. However, the U.S. contribution to
IDA is being tightened up because of the balance of
payments problem. In addition, the European Economic Community nations refuse to assist the U.S.
balance of payments problem by allowing more IDA
funds to be tied to U.S. purchases by LDC's.[32]
Thus, it appears that new patterns and/or methodology in dispensing aid multilaterally must be
forthcoming.

NEW TRENDS IN WORLD AID

Bilateral and multilateral aid has shifted
from the reconstruction era of the first decade
after World War II to assistance of the LDC's in
their struggles to increase their standard of
living. Economic development has replaced reconstruction as the major goal of world aid.

The World Bank Group has made some changes in
industry emphasis during the period since the War.
Its direction has been on lending for electric
power and transportation but in recent years, more
World Bank emphasis has been toward development of
agriculture, industry, and education. IFC's early
emphasis was on mining and manufacturing companies

and assistance to private development finance companies. However, IFC has invested recently in new areas such as food processing, distribution services, a public utility, and tourism. IDA has emphasized somewhat the same projects as the World Bank.[33] In other words, the World Bank and IDA have placed emphasis on the basic elements of social overhead capital but with an increasing interest on agriculture.

The major emphasis of bilateral aid in the decade after World War II was for reconstruction purposes. The Marshall Plan program was a prime example of such aid. However, since the mid-1950's, bilateral aid has concentrated on economic development. In recent years, this aid has been concentrated on fewer recipient nations with more emphasis on making as a condition of aid disbursement, the purchasing of needed machinery and commodities from the donor nation. Thus, the indirect result has been to subsidize the private sector of the donor countries.

There has also been a trend in the industrialized nations to channel more aid appropriations through multilateral agencies such as those of the World Bank Group. This aid is given without political conditions attached.

In summary, the trends in direction and method of disbursement of world aid have been changing over the last few years. More aid is being channeled through multilateral agencies. Bilateral aid has decreased, is being concentrated among fewer recipient nations, and is becoming relatively more tied to purchase of the donor country's goods. Relatively more aid is being directed at private enterprise, e.g., the IFC operations, private development finance companies, tourism, and services. The agribusiness industry is obtaining more and more interest of the aid agencies and industrialized donor countries. The LDC's are practicing more and better national planning of their economies and, thus, are utilizing aid more efficiently.

THE FUTURE OF WORLD AID[34]

The United Nations' goal of 1 per cent of industrialized nations' GNP as an annual official appropriation to the LDC's--approximately $15 billion in 1968--is an admirable goal. However, only $6 billion has been forthcoming and it is very doubtful that the LDC's could even absorb $15 billion per year. In addition, the rising population growth rates cancel out much of the economic growth of these nations. The world is unable to feed adequately its 3 billion inhabitants in 1968, and U.N. forecasts reveal that the world's population may be 6 billion by the year 2000.

Thus, a number of objectives, some already being implemented, must be initiated or continued if the LDC's are to benefit from world aid. First, the trend away from bilateral and toward multilateral aid must be accelerated so that fewer politically entangling agreements will envolve the LDC's.

Second, aid agencies should continue the trend to channeling more aid to the private enterprise sector of LDC's. Private enterprise in the LDC's can be the dynamic and catalytic agent for initiating change. The entrepreneurial capacity of the LDC's is quite limited; thus, development of this sector through world aid may lead to dynamic changes greatly beneficial to the LDC's. More world assistance of this area can be generated by placing an increasing emphasis on IFC investments. The World Bank can increase its lending to IFC for the purpose of making possible greater IFC investments in private enterprise. The regional development banks in Latin America, Africa, and Asia can also increase investment activities toward the private sector. More and bigger dams and electric power-producing facilities can be built by social overhead capital projects financed by world aid, but if sufficient private enterprise does not exist to plug into these facilities, their construction may be in vain.

Third, agribusiness--an old industry with a modern name--must be greatly expanded if the world's vastly increasing population is to be fed. Some local public financing is needed for this industry but the management and ownership is basically private in nature. Agribusiness consists of the fertilizer producers, machinery manufacturers, credit institutions, and food processors all of which combine to plant, harvest, process, and distribute products which feed the world's population.[35]

Fourth, world aid must be channeled to those service industries in LDC's which will generate not only foreign exchange savings but which will also earn foreign exchange. Such an industry is tourism. Many of the underdeveloped countries have new international airports and all of them have exotic tourist attractions. As the developed countries limit travels in other developed nations because of balance of payments problems, the LDC's stand to benefit from a well-developed tourist industry. Again, the regional development banks and IFC can be instrumental in developing the tourist sector of LDC's.

Finally, attitudes must change toward foreign economic assistance among the peoples of the industrialized nations of the world, and especially among legislators. John Adler, of the World Bank, believes the broad popular support for aid is on moral grounds, as witnessed by massive aid collected and disseminated by churches and non-profit agencies such as CARE. The legislative support for aid has been on grounds of mutual security, but must now be changed to an emphasis on moral grounds.[36]

AGRIBUSINESS

Because of the vastly important needs for satisfying the world's food requirements, probably no other industrial sector may be as important as agribusiness. Therefore, a more extensive analysis of this area is necessary. Much research is being done and the literature is growing. Agribusiness

departments are being organized in some of the
leading universities of the United States. A number
of reports and articles expound on the necessity of
increasing agricultural production.[37] The First
International Agribusiness Conference, sponsored by
the Chicago Board of Trade, was held in Chicago,
May 10-12, 1967, as an attempt to bring together a
large number of experts concerned with the world's
agricultural problems. William S. Gaud, Administrator of the U.S. Agency for International Development, calls this growing emphasis on agribusiness:
"The Green Revolution."[38]

Among the various aspects of agribusiness, the
production of fertilizer probably is the most
important because a very rapid gain in agricultural
output is possible with efficient use of fertilizer.[39]
In addition, it has been forecast that the LDC's
will need to increase their food production by
nearly two thirds by 1985 to keep pace with their
population growth.[40] To produce this increased
output, these nations will have to increase by tenfold their consumption of fertilizer by 1985.[41]
The LDC's accounted for 8.5 per cent of the world's
fertilizer consumption in 1957, 15 per cent in 1966,
and should account for 20 per cent in 1970 and one
third in 1980.[42] Martin Rosen, in his address to
the National Industrial Conference Board's National
Convocation on World Hunger,[43] states that private
entrepreneurs must produce the raw materials needed
for fertilizer production in the countries where
they are found, then transport these materials to
LDC's, which will purchase and use fertilizer, and
finally, construct fertilizer production facilities
in these LDC's.

The engineering problem for producing fertilizer is quite complex. The raw materials are
hydrocarbons--which are petrochemical products,
and phosphate and potash. These materials are
found in many LDC's but seldom together. The
secret to success in greatly increasing fertilizer
production among the LDC's is to know where and how
to produce, how to transport the raw materials, and
what marketing systems to establish.[44] Thus, a

complex integrated system from raw materials producer to final consumer must be organized.

The technological progress in designing and
constructing fertilizer manufacturing facilities
has led to greater economies of scale in the LDC's,
especially in recent years. In 1962, a plant for
producing ammonia, one of the necessary ingredients
of fertilizer, generally had a daily capacity of no
more than 300 tons. In 1967, plants with daily
capacity of 600 to 1,500 tons were being built or
designed.[45] Thus, capital cost of fertilizer output and lower fertilizer prices for farmers have
been made possible.[46]

In addition to technological progress in construction, new and larger refrigerated tankers make
possible more economic transportation of ammonia.
The increasing expansion of the petrochemical
industry in countries such as Nigeria, Venezuela,
and those of the Persian Gulf area can furnish the
needed increase in ammonia production which may
then be transported to LDC's which are in great
need of fertilizer.

The importance of investment in such manufacturing facilities is demonstrated by the large
foreign exchange costs of LDC's in satisfying their
fertilizer requirements. This cost was estimated
in 1965 to be $825 million.[47] In many cases, the
foreign exchange cost of fertilizer alone is 20 per
cent or more of the LDC's export earnings. India,
in 1963, had unused supplies of fertilizer piled in
warehouses. Over four years later, 20 per cent of
India's foreign exchange earnings are being used to
import fertilizer or the raw materials to make it.[48]

Martin Rosen of IFC presented an example of
construction in an LDC of a nitrogen plant with an
annual capacity of 200,000 tons. Foreign exchange
required for a plant of this size would amount to
$35-40 million. On the contrary, the imported cost
of bulk nitrogen is approximately $200 per ton.
With the plant operating at only 75 per cent of
capacity, the foreign exchange savings generated

from such an operation would be about $30 million a year.[49] This represents a very good return on an investment of this kind.

Thus, the area of fertilizer production is one of great importance to the LDC's. This industry is predominantly privately owned in nature. Many traditional and political problems must be eliminated before integrated multilateral operations of the magnitude described in this section will become accepted and practiced in a widespread manner. Vast economic resources must be jointly combined through cooperation among private investors, international corporations, and the governments of both the industrialized nations and the LDC's.

CONCLUSIONS

The changing patterns of international flows of official assistance to LDC's has been described in this chapter. Some significant trends have been discussed. Perhaps the most significant of these trends concern the emphasis on multilateral aid, investment in the private sector, and the increasing recognition of the problem of world food requirements of a greatly increasing population.

One international institution exists which can do much to facilitate these trends in aid patterns and help alleviate some of the problems heretofore discussed. That institution is the International Finance Corporation (IFC), founded in 1956 as a member of the World Bank Group. IFC is a multilateral international financial institution which invests in private enterprise projects in member LDC's without government guarantee. And IFC has begun to place greater emphasis on investment in projects in the agribusiness sector.

The remainder of this book will analyze the evolution of IFC, its administration, operations, and functions, its procedures for project evaluation and reporting of financial operations, and its problems. Fifteen case studies of projects in

which IFC has invested will be analyzed. Although
the emphasis of the book will be on IFC's first
decade of operations, 1956-1966, an attempt will
be made to predict the future direction of the
institution's operations.

CHAPTER **2** ORIGIN AND
BACKGROUND OF THE
INTERNATIONAL
FINANCE CORPORATION

INTRODUCTION

The conception and evolution of the International Finance Corporation (IFC) began indirectly in 1944 at the United Nations Monetary and Financial Conference, Bretton Woods, New Hampshire. This conference was attended by more than two dozen nations of the world. One of the major topics discussed was the financial problem involving reconstruction of war-torn countries after the war's end. Some institutional machinery was necessary to channel funds from able to needy countries so that this reconstruction could be facilitated. Such an institution, The International Bank for Reconstruction and Development (IBRD), or World Bank, had its origin at the Bretton Woods Conference.

The articles of IBRD were signed by twenty-eight governments on December 27, 1945, and the Bank's doors were opened for business on June 25, 1946.[1] Its primary business, at first, was making loans to European countries for reconstruction purposes. Since 1948, the Bank has placed almost its entire emphasis on lending to less-developed countries. The major development projects financed by the World Bank in these countries have been electric power, transportation, communications, agriculture, forestry, and industry.

The IBRD thoroughly scrutinizes proposed projects and finances no projects which are not guaranteed by the host government. Its loans are generally made for periods of fifteen years and carry relatively high rates of interest, generally 5.5 to 6 per cent. Financial resources of the IBRD consist of subscribed capital from member countries, World Bank bond issues, repayments of earlier loans, net earnings, and sales of parts of loans to other investors.

The World Bank represented a large step forward in channeling development funds to less-developed countries. However, in the late 1940's, a gap in the system was recognized. Relatively little private investment was going into underdeveloped areas. Except where investment is completely state-controlled, the factor adding dynamism to economic development is generally regarded as private investment. The private enterprise sector in these countries needed capital and the World Bank was unable to furnish it.

Two charter limitations made impossible greater participation by the Bank in the private sectors of underdeveloped countries. First, the Bank was precluded from lending to projects which were not government guaranteed and, secondly, the Bank was not allowed to invest in equity capital of proposed projects. Discussions began among officials of the United Nations, the IBRD, and the United States government about methods for expanding the institutional machinery to fill this gap.

THE PROPOSAL AND ITS ACCEPTANCE

Although the concept of IFC was present at the 1944 Bretton Woods Conference,[2] the idea was not advanced because participants were in favor of granting broader powers to the World Bank. However, discussion of the concept began to take place. During the late 1940's, officials of the IBRD recognized the limitations facing the World Bank and began privately to discuss the idea of IFC.

In President Truman's inaugural address of
January 20, 1949, he set forth his Point Four
program from which evolved American policy toward
economic development and which, as B.E. Matecki
puts it, "placed the policy of the United States
on a plane of high principle"[3] with regard to
economic development. And in 1946, the United
Nations Economic and Social Council instructed the
Economic and Employment Commission to initiate a
Subcommission on Economic Development.[4] This
subcommission held sessions in 1947 and 1948
during which general methods for financing economic
development were discussed. During the third session of this group in 1949, a "United Nations Economic Development Administration" (UNEDA) was proposed. This agency was to finance low-yield projects which were not self-liquidating and member
countries were to contribute to the agency's capital.

During 1950, two events occurred which aided
the IFC idea. The UNEDA concept failed to be endorsed by the Subcommission on Economic Development
during its fourth session and the Gray Report was
issued. The Gray Report was requested by President
Truman and set forth proposals for American activity
in economic development, including a program of
basic aid to underdeveloped nations for which an
appropriation of $500 million was proposed. Presi-
dent Truman requested the U.S. International Development Advisory Board, headed by Nelson Rockefeller,
to consider the Gray proposals and design a strategy
for employing American resources.

On March 7, 1951, the Development Advisory
Board submitted its report entitled Partners in
Progress, which was popularly referred to as the
"Rockefeller Report." The report was written
during a national emergency just proclaimed because
of the Korean War. Because of this fact, the report
emphasized international economic development as
being in the best interests of U.S. defense policy.
The Rockefeller Report endorsed the Gray Report's
proposals of large expenditures for economic development and placed great emphasis on private investment. However, the report did propose an "Inter-

national Development Authority" to finance some
public works in less developed countries with the
United States to contribute about $200 million to
the agency.

The report proposed tax incentives, bilateral
tax and commercial treaties, underwriting of transfer risks on foreign dollar obligations and other
measures designed to encourage the flow of private
investment to the less-developed nations. The
report also recommended the establishment of an
International Finance Corporation to be associated
with the World Bank. This institution would be
authorized to make loans in local and foreign cur-
rencies to private enterprise without government
guarantee and to make nonvoting equity investments
in these enterprises in participation with local
private investors. The IFC proposal called for
authorized capital of $400 million and a U.S. con-
tribution as high as $150 million. The IFC would
utilize the management and staff of the World Bank.
The report suggested that the United States take
the initiative in developing the institution.

In May, 1951, the United Nations Economic,
Employment and Development Commission recommended
to the Economic and Social Council (ECOSOC) that
the proposal be considered. In August, 1951, the
Council debated the issue and then adopted Resolution No. 368 (XIII), which requested the World Bank
to decide what an International Finance Corporation
could contribute to the existing economic development financing institutions.

The World Bank, after deliberation of the
ECOSOC request, published a "Report on the Proposal
for an International Finance Corporation" in April,
1952. This report discussed the need for such an
institution and its possible role and potentiali-
ties. The report also set forth some basic principles of operation and organization. Some of the
views of the Rockefeller Report were borrowed.

Meanwhile, the United States, at first,
opposed the IFC through negative stands by the

Treasury Department, Federal Reserve System, and
Export-Import Bank. A major reason for this oppr-
sition was the belief that a multinational agency
should not hold an equity interest in private business firms.[5] Such a practice involved a business-
government partnership and this was opposed to American economic standards. It was further believed
that the IFC might jeopardize World Bank and Export-
Import Bank lending operations. A third reason for
U.S. Treasury Department reaction to the proposal
was the suggested $150 million U.S. contribution
and the effect of this upon the Eisenhower Administration's budget-balancing policies.

Among other U.S. governmental agencies' attitudes toward the IFC proposal were those of the
State Department and its lukewarm and qualified
support. The Securities and Exchange Commission
was one of the few agencies which gave the proposal
its whole-hearted support.

Within the business community, differences of
opinion arose. The National Foreign Trade Council
opposed the IFC proposal because its members sup-
posedly believed that international economic development should be accomplished by private enterprise.
This viewpoint was stated and reiterated at the
Conventions of the National Foreign Trade Council
in 1952, 1953, and 1954.

However, there is some indication from the
later public hearings on the Congressional bill to
establish the IFC that some business organizations
did support the proposal. Among these were the
American Farm Bureau Federation, the American
Bankers Association, and the United States Council
of the International Chamber of Commerce.[6]

In May, 1953, the World Bank issued a report
to ECOSOC on the status of the IFC proposal.[7] The
essence of this report was that: 1) the U.S.
stalemate still existed, 2) most underdeveloped
countries supported IFC, 3) a few industrialized
nations supported IFC, 4) some industrialized nations were unable to contribute to an IFC at that

time, and 5) the World Bank had noted mixed opin-
ions toward IFC from the business community.

On June 3, 1954, the World Bank submitted a
Second Report on the Status of the Proposal for an
International Finance Corporation.[8] The status of
the proposal remained as it had at the time of the
1953 report.

During the Summer of 1954, the U.N. members
began discussing the Special United Nations Fund
for Economic Development (SUNFED). This agency was
proposed to finance investments which were not self-
liquidating and which were nonyielding. Underdeveloped countries began to espouse both SUNFED
and IFC.

The World Bank had kept the IFC concept alive,
but more and more support was being given to the
SUNFED idea. The pressure mounted against the
United States' opposition to IFC. As late as
October 25, 1954, the U.S. position remained un-
changed.[9] However, on November 11, 1954, Treasury
Secretary George Humphrey announced in a surprise
declaration that the National Advisory Council
would ask for Congressional approval of United
States membership in an established International
Finance Corporation.[10]

The abrupt change in the U.S. position was
very surprising. Several reasons may have caused
this change. The U.S. position came closer to
supporting IFC than it did SUNFED. The U.S. government probably did not wish to support both institutions at this time. Officials from IBRD may have
persuaded U.S. officials during private conversations to advocate approval of IFC.

England and Canada then changed their positions
and the IFC appeared to be assured of establishment.
Finally, on December 11, 1954, the U.N. General
Assembly endorsed the IFC concept by a vote of 50
to 0 and requested the World Bank to establish IFC.[11]

FORMATION OF THE IFC

After the U.N. General Assembly vote, the
World Bank transmitted, on April 11, 1955, articles
of agreement of the International Finance Corporation to member governments for their deliberation
and approval. Capitalization of the IFC was to be
$100 million and, since the United States' share
was to be $35,168,000, approval of the articles of
agreement by the U.S. Congress was mandatory for
the success of the proposal.

On May 2, 1955, President Eisenhower recommended to the U.S. Congress that legislation be
passed permitting the membership of the United
States in IFC. His comments were as follows:

> The entire free world needs capital to
> provide a sound basis for economic growth
> which will support rising standards of
> living and will fortify free social and
> political institutions. Action to that
> end by cooperating nations is essential.
>
> In its own enlightened self-interest,
> the United States is vitally concerned
> that capital should move into productive
> activities in free countries unable to
> finance development needs out of their
> own resources.
>
> Government funds cannot, and should
> not, be regarded as the basic sources of
> capital for international investment. The
> best means is investment by private indivi-
> duals and enterprises. The major purpose
> of the new institution, consequently, will
> be to help channel private capital and ex-
> perienced and competent private management
> into productive investment opportunities
> that would not otherwise be developed.
> Through the Corporation we can cooperate
> more effectively with other people for
> mutual prosperity and expanding interna-
> tional trade, thus contributing to the
> peace and the solidarity of the free world.[12]

Hearings in Congress began during the Summer of 1955 before a subcommittee of the Senate Committee on Banking and Currency for S. 1894, and by the House Committee on Banking and Currency for H.R. 6228, both bills asking for American support and participation in IFC.

One of the earlier proposals for IFC was that IFC should make capital stock investments. However, the articles of agreement did not give IFC the power to make such investments. IFC could make so-called venture capital investments but could not take capital stock in return. According to the explanatory memorandum on the proposed articles of agreement of IFC which were submitted during the hearings on S. 1894, IFC would be expected, in cases in which an investor would normally take an equity position, to require a participation in the profits of the company financed and a right, exercisable by any purchaser of the investment from IFC, to subscribe to, or to convert the investment into, capital shares.[13]

During the Senate committee hearings, Secretary of Treasury George Humphrey stated,

> When the IFC project was first talked about, investment in equities was one of the proposed methods of operations. We in the Treasury did not think it would be desirable or feasible for an international governmental corporation to invest in common stock and to take the management responsibility which stock ownership entails. The present plan has eliminated the equity investment and management feature. The administration believes this is a great improvement and supports the project fully in its present form.[14]

This statement by the Secretary of Treasury seems to be the public justification for the last-minute support of IFC by the United States government.

During the hearings on IFC in Congress, officials of the Treasury Department, State Department,
and U.S. Export-Import Bank testified in support of
approval of IFC. The Securities and Exchange Commission issued a statement that the proposed IFC
financing activities and methods did not appear to
be in conflict with any U.S. securities law. Supporting testimony was also heard from officials of
the United States Council of the International
Chamber of Commerce, the Investment Bankers Association of America, the Washington Board of Trade,
the American Farm Bureau Federation, and the American Bankers Association. The National Foreign
Trade Council and the American Paper and Pulp Association seemed to be the only large groups to voice
opposition. The Chairman of the Senate subcommittee
pointed out that many of the members of the National
Foreign Trade Council were also members of the
United States Council of the International Chamber
of Commerce.[15] The latter agency had voiced strong
support for IFC and the implication was strong that
the NFTC's process of policy-making in the IFC case
could be questioned.

Among the committee members, only Senator
Homer E. Capehart, an Indiana Republican, seemed to
question strongly the necessity for an International
Finance Corporation. His questioning of witnesses
seemed to imply a belief that an American institution could do such financing as was proposed for
IFC just as efficiently as an international institution. He seemed to advocate that the U.S. Export-
Import Bank could be empowered to do anything which
IFC might do. Actually IFC's operations were meant
to augment any export-financing operations of the
U.S. Export-Import Bank. Apparently, his views
were not very influential, because the President of
the United States was authorized to accept membership in and subscribe to the capital of the IFC by
the International Finance Corporation Act, approved
by Congress on August 11, 1955.[16] On December 5,
1955, the United States delivered its instrument of
acceptance to the World Bank. The official date of
birth of the IFC was July 24, 1956. A total of 31
countries, with total subscriptions of $78.4 mil-

lion, had deposited their notices of acceptance by
that date.

CONCLUSIONS

A new international financial institution to
assist in world economic development had been established. The idea had originated in the World
Bank because Bank officials recognized the financing
limitations imposed on the Bank by its charter,
especially in the area of financing private enterprise in underdeveloped countries without government guarantee. Bank officials believed these
limitations could not be eliminated without establishment of a separate institution.

The approval of the IFC by the United States
was mandatory because without American capital, the
institution would not have been able to function.
American policies toward economic development were
quite similar to World Bank policy. However, the
U.S. government opposed IFC from the beginning.
Only when the World Bank dropped the equity investment proposal from the IFC methods of financing did
the United States offer its support.

B.E. Matecki suggests that an international
agency actually may have persuaded U.S. government
officials to formulate foreign policy which included
support of the IFC proposal.[17] This may be true
especially in light of the easy access for close
communications between World Bank and U.S. government officials in Washington. Both the IBRD and
the American administration compromised their
positions and this action led to American support.
Furthermore, United Nations members, especially
Latin Americans, were increasing their support of
SUNFED and other proposed institutions which were
public financing agencies in nature. American opposition to this type institution was far greater
than its opposition to IFC. Some institution was
going to be established. Therefore, the Eisenhower
administration, strongly in favor of private enterprise, decided IFC could more closely represent the
desires of the United States.

CHAPTER **3** OPERATIONS AND
ADMINISTRATION OF THE
INTERNATIONAL
FINANCE CORPORATION

PURPOSE

The IFC was established for the following general purpose, as stated in the Articles of Agreement:

> The purpose of the Corporation is to further economic development by encouraging the growth of productive private enterprise in member countries, particularly in the less developed areas, thus supplementing the activities of the International Bank for Reconstruction and Development.[1]

To facilitate achievement of this purpose, the Articles of Agreement commissioned IFC to:

> 1. in association with private investors, assist in financing the establishment, improvement and expansion of productive private enterprise which would contribute to the development of its member countries by making investments, without guarantee of repayment by the member government concerned, in cases where sufficient private capital is not available on reasonable terms;

2.   seek to bring together investment
opportunities, domestic and foreign
private capital, and experienced
management; and

3.   seek to stimulate, and to help create
conditions conducive to the flow of
private capital, domestic and foreign,
into productive investment in member
countries.[2]

The IFC performs several functions in fulfilling these objectives. In addition to financing
private industrial projects without government
guarantee, IFC may also agree to underwrite securities issued by business firms. IFC assists in
encouraging financial institutions in capital
exporting countries to participate in industrial
development in the less developed countries by
selling them investments from its own portfolio.
Furthermore, IFC finances private development finance companies whose capital is then invested in
private enterprise. Finally, IFC performs a number
of miscellaneous activities in the industrial development finance area, among these the appraisal of
investment proposals submitted to the World Bank
Group by industrial and mining companies, the advising of management of companies in which IFC has
invested, and assistance in drafting market surveys.
These functions will be analyzed in depth in this
chapter.

MEMBERSHIP AND CAPITAL

Only members of the World Bank are eligible
for membership in IFC. Original capital of $100
million was authorized in the form of 100,000
shares having a par value of $1,000 each. Table
1 shows the number of shares and amount available
for subscription by member countries at the time of
establishment of IFC. The United States has the
largest number of shares with 35,168 and Panama has
the least number with two shares.[3]

Countries which were not charter members were given the privilege to become members subsequent to December 31, 1956, and, for the purpose of enabling such subsequent memberships, the capital stock of IFC may be increased, with majority vote of members, by as much as 10,000 shares.[4]

The IFC was established on July 24, 1956, when 31 countries, having subscribed to capital of $78 million, had submitted instruments of acceptance of the Articles of Agreement. On September 10, 1956, just prior to the Inaugural Meeting of the Board of Governors of IFC, the institution had 51 members, whose subscriptions amounted to $92 million.[5] On January 4, 1967, Guyana became the 83rd member of IFC. Guyana's subscription brought member countries' subscriptions to $99,929,000.[6]

ORGANIZATION AND ADMINISTRATION

Article IV of the Articles of Agreement provides for a Board of Governors, a Board of Directors, a Chairman of the Board of Directors, a President, and such other officers as are needed to enable the IFC to fulfill its objectives. The members of the World Bank's Board of Governors and Board of Executive Directors are empowered to be ex officio the same officers in IFC, if the countries which they represent in the World Bank become members of IFC. The President of the World Bank is empowered to be Chairman of the Board of Directors of IFC. The President of IFC is appointed upon the advice of the Chairman and with the approval of the Board of Directors. All powers of IFC are vested in the Board of Governors. Some IFC functions may be carried out by World Bank officers who act in a similar capacity for both organizations. For instance, the Office of Information and its Director function for both the World Bank and IFC. The principle involved is to utilize, where possible, World Bank officials in IFC operations in order to eliminate unnecessary administrative overhead. The offices of IFC are located at the same address in Washington, D.C., as are those of the World Bank.

Table 1

Subscriptions to Capital Stock of the
International Finance Corporation
at Its Establishment

Country	Number of Shares	Amount (in U.S. dollars)
Australia	2,215	2,215,000
Austria	554	554,000
Belgium	2,492	2,492,000
Bolivia	78	78,000
Brazil	1,163	1,163,000
Burma	166	166,000
Canada	3,600	3,600,000
Ceylon	166	166,000
Chile	388	388,000
China	6,646	6,646,000
Colombia	388	388,000
Costa Rica	22	22,000
Cuba	388	388,000
Denmark	753	753,000
Dominican Republic	22	22,000
Ecuador	35	35,000
Egypt	590	590,000
El Salvador	11	11,000
Ethiopia	33	33,000
Finland	421	421,000
France	5,815	5,815,000
Germany	3,655	3,655,000
Greece	277	277,000
Guatemala	22	22,000
Haiti	22	22,000
Honduras	11	11,000
Iceland	11	11,000
India	4,431	4,431,000
Indonesia	1,218	1,218,000
Iran	372	372,000
Iraq	67	67,000

Country	Number of Shares	Amount (in U.S. dollars)
Israel	50	50,000
Italy	1,994	1,994,000
Japan	2,769	2,769,000
Jordan	33	33,000
Lebanon	50	50,000
Luxembourg	111	111,000
Mexico	720	720,000
Netherlands	3,046	3,046,000
Nicaragua	9	9,000
Norway	554	554,000
Pakistan	1,108	1,108,000
Panama	2	2,000
Paraguay	16	16,000
Peru	194	194,000
Philippines	166	166,000
Sweden	1,108	1,108,000
Syria	72	72,000
Thailand	139	139,000
Turkey	476	476,000
Union of South Africa	1,108	1,108,000
United Kingdom	14,400	14,400,000
United States	35,168	35,168,000
Uruguay	116	116,000
Venezuela	116	116,000
Yugoslavia	443	443,000
Total	100,000	100,000,000

Source: Articles of Agreement of the International
Finance Corporation, Washington, D.C.,
July 20, 1956, pp. 26-27.

However, IFC funds are kept separate from World
Bank funds.

Each member of IFC has 250 votes plus one for
each share of stock held. Thus, the United States
has 35,418 votes compared with Panama which has 252
votes. Since most matters of business are decided
by a majority vote, the United States, the United
Kingdom with 14,650 votes, and one other country
together could very well control any vote. Thus,
the importance and power of the United States'
participation in IFC is demonstrated.

Although IFC was authorized to share personnel
and facilities in its operations, it was not originally authorized to borrow from or lend to the
World Bank. However, amendment of the Articles of
Agreement in 1965 enabled IFC to borrow from the
World Bank. This amendment will be discussed in
more detail in a later section.

FINANCIAL RESOURCES AND HOW THEY ARE OBTAINED

Original capital stock authorized by the
Articles of Agreement was $100 million. Article II,
Section 2, authorized an increase in the capital
stock of IFC of $10 million for the purpose of faci-
litating new memberships subsequent to the charter
memberships. This additional capital could be authorized by a majority vote of the Board of Governors. In April, 1963, the Board of Directors recommended to the Board of Governors a $10 million
increase and the increase was approved.[7] Guyana's
membership in IFC in January, 1967, brought subscribed capital to $99,929,000.

In addition to subscribed and paid-in capital,
IFC has other financial resources available.
Earnings from its investments as well as sales of
some of its holdings to other financial institutions give IFC a further source of funds, in addition to the institution's ability to borrow. These
funds have enabled IFC to commit its resources to
100 enterprises in thirty-four countries in the

amount of $173 million during the first ten years
of operations.[8]

Among the operational principles set forth in
the Articles of Agreement is the following:

> the Corporation shall seek to revolve its
> funds by selling its investments to pri-
> vate investors whenever it can appro-
> priately do so on satisfactory terms.[9]

IFC has implemented this principle during the first
ten years by selling loan and equity investments
totaling $34.8 million in fifty enterprises located
in twenty-six countries. These investments have
been sold to private investors and financial institutions in the United States, Europe, and the
Middle East.[10] IFC's tenth annual report points
out that about 50 per cent of its sales of investments have been concentrated in only four countries:
Brazil, Colombia, Mexico, and Peru; whereas about
38 per cent of IFC's portfolio investments are located in Argentina, Colombia, India, and Pakistan.[11]
The implication is that private foreign investors
are more favorable toward such Latin American countries as Mexico and Brazil than toward investments
in the Asian subcontinent. Perhaps a reason for
this is that the former investments are much more
seasoned than those made in India and Pakistan.
Furthermore, the climate for private investment may
be more favorable in Latin America than in India
and Pakistan.

In addition to the sales of investments by IFC,
the institution has closed out investments amounting
to $21.5 million located in twelve countries. These
are primarily loan investments in which the principal has been repaid.[12] These funds have been
available for investment in new projects.

The IFC has earned interest and dividend income on its investments and has made net profits on
the sale of its investments to other private investors. These funds are set aside in a Reserve
Against Losses. On June 30, 1966, this reserve

account amounted to $28,367,887, including net in-
come on investments during the tenth fiscal year of
$4,364,489.[13] These funds are not ordinarily used
for reinvestment but will be available to cover any
losses which might occur.

Finally, IFC is permitted to borrow funds.
The original Articles of Agreement authorized IFC
to "borrow funds, and...to furnish such collateral...
as it shall determine."[14] This authorized IFC to
issue its own debt obligations; however, the institution never has availed itself of this opportunity.
The principal reason given for this was that one of
the primary sources of operational funds of the
World Bank has been the issue of World Bank bonds.
Officials of IFC, who are also officials of the
World Bank, believed that borrowing by IFC might
jeopardize the marketability of World Bank bonds.
Thus, no borrowing has been done by IFC by issuing
debt obligations on the open market.

During the September, 1964, Annual Meeting of
the Board of Governors of IFC in Tokyo, the Board
stated that an increase in IFC's financial resources
would be necessary within a few years because of the
increased investment activity projected for the institution. Such an increase would be necessary to
enable IFC to fulfill its purposes as stated in the
Articles of Agreement.

A change in the Articles was recommended to
enable the World Bank to lend funds to IFC in a
manner similar to World Bank financing of private
investment finance companies. The Board of Directors of the World Bank and IFC recommended the
Articles of Agreement of IFC and the Bank be
changed to permit IFC to borrow from the Bank an
amount not to exceed four times the unimpaired subscribed capital and surplus of IFC.[15] During 1965,
member governments approved the change. Hearings
were held on H.R. 8816 in the U.S. House of Representatives and on S. 1742 in the U.S. Senate. Both
Houses passed these bills and the President of the
United States signed into law an act enabling the
U.S. Governor of IFC to approve the change. Late

in 1965, the Articles were amended, allowing IFC to
borrow up to approximately $400 million from the
World Bank.

Thus IFC now has over $500 million available
for potential investment. In the past, IFC's
largest investments have been about $6 million.
The authorization for IFC to borrow from the World
Bank will add much flexibility to IFC's operations
and should enable it to invest as much as $15-20 mil-
lion in a single project. With such resources, IFC
will be able to further diversify its portfolio.

USES OF FINANCIAL RESOURCES

The IFC was founded for the primary purpose of
providing financial assistance to private enterprise in less-developed countries. It does so, as
empowered by its charter, by investing its funds in
private enterprises without the guarantee of the
host government. No investment will be made in a
project which is guaranteed by the host government,
or in which the government has a significant investment, nor will an investment be made in any country
where the government in power does not welcome such
international financing for its privately-owned
companies. Investments are possible only in member
countries and any country which is not a member of
the World Bank cannot be a member of IFC.

Certain guiding principles for IFC investment
operations are outlined in the Articles of Agreement.[16] They are as follows:

> 1. The Corporation shall not undertake
> any financing for which, in its opinion,
> sufficient private capital could be ob-
> tained on reasonable terms;
>
> 2. The Corporation shall not finance
> an enterprise in the territories of any
> member if the member objects to such
> financing;

3.   The Corporation shall impose no conditions that the proceeds of any new financing by it shall be spent in the
territories of any particular country;

4.   The Corporation shall not assume
responsibility for managing any enterprise
in which it has invested;

5.   The Corporation shall undertake its
financing on terms and conditions which
it considers appropriate, taking into
account the requirements of the enterprise, the risks being undertaken by the
Corporation, and the terms and conditions
normally obtained by private investors
for similar financing;

6.   The Corporation shall seek to revolve
its funds by selling its investments to
private investors whenever it can appro-
priately do so on satisfactory terms;

7.   The Corporation shall seek to maintain a reasonable diversification in its
investments.

Two types of private capital are necessary for
industrial growth: business, or working, capital
and investment, or long-term, capital. IFC fur-
nishes both types of capital and its investments
act as the catalyst which encourages local and foreign investors to commit the majority of the funds
for each project. According to the 1965-1966
Annual Report, IFC has participated in the financing
of projects whose estimated total capital cost has
been $675 million. This does not include IFC com-
mitments in private development finance companies.
Of this total amount, IFC's share (net of cancellations and terminations) has been $140 million; local
sources have invested $330 million; and foreign in-
vestors have committed $205 million.[17] Thus, for
every dollar of IFC investment in these projects,
other sources contribute nearly four dollars. In a
later section of this chapter, IFC operations in

the area of financing private development finance
companies will be analyzed. This is a further use
of funds which creates an added multiplier effect
in the less developed countries.

When first established, IFC was prohibited
from making investments in the capital stock of an
enterprise. However, its investments were not conventional fixed-interest debt obligations. Some
features of both equity and debt were present in
these early investments. The term used by the IFC
to describe the equity feature in these investments
was "venture capital." Some investments were long-
term loans with the right to share in the profits
of the company. Other loans carried the option to
subscribe to share capital. Still other loans were
convertible into capital shares. IFC could not
exercise either stock option or conversion features
of these loans but such loans could be sold to private investors who could exercise such options.
These features made IFC's investments more marketable before 1961.

During the first five years of operations, IFC
officials recognized that the prohibition against
equity investments severely hampered IFC's potential
in fulfilling its objectives. On February 24, 1961,
the President of IFC announced a desire to amend
the Articles of Agreement to permit the institution's investment in share capital. This resolution
was presented to the Board of Governors. In the
United States, authorization for the American governor to approve the resolution was considered in
H.R. 6765 and S. 1648 in the House and Senate respectively.[18] Secretary of Treasury Douglas Dillon,
in testimony before the Subcommittee No. 1 of the
House Committee on Banking and Currency, presented
two important reasons for the necessity of the
amendment. First, the use of convertible debentures by IFC created problems because investors in
foreign capital markets, especially those in less
developed countries, were not very familiar with
such an investment instrument. Secondly, the use
of long-term stock options required complex legal
problems, especially in the negotiating stages.[19]

Thus, after short hearings, the United States voted
authorization for the change. The amendment was
approved by IFC's Board of Governors in September,
1961.

IFC's first investment in capital shares where
the equity investment was part of the initial commitment was made in February, 1962, when the institution made its first investment in Spain. This
was part of a $3 million investment in Fabrica Es-
pañola Magnetos, S.A. (FEMSA), a family business
and leading Spanish manufacturer of automotive
electrical equipment. IFC purchased 30 million
pesetas in common shares (about $500,000). This
investment will be discussed in more detail in
Chapter 8.[20] Since its first direct equity investment in 1962, IFC has invested, or agreed to invest,
in equity in fifty-two enterprises located in
twenty-seven countries and, at the end of fiscal
year 1966, IFC's total portfolio of $84 million was
composed of $28.9 million in shares, or about one
third of the portfolio.[21]

This amendment has facilitated IFC's operations
in two other areas. It has aided IFC's investments
in private development finance companies. IFC now
owns shares in seventeen such companies in fifteen
countries.[22] The sale of investments from IFC's
portfolio also has been aided by this change. IFC's
underwriting and standby activities in share capital
investments will be discussed in a later section of
this chapter.

The terms of repayment of loans and the interest
rates are matters of negotiation between IFC and the
enterprise. In fact, the investment agreement between IFC and the firm is kept strictly confiden-
tial. IFC has no standard terms and negotiates
terms which are appropriate for the company concerned as well as for economic and money market
conditions in the host country. IFC does charge a
commitment fee of 1 per cent per annum on the
undisbursed portion of its investment. Length of
maturity for IFC loans ranges from five to fifteen
years. The Corporation also generally mixes its

investments between straight loan and equity arrangements.

IFC's early investments were principally in industrial and mining projects. Investments have been made in: steel companies in Argentina, Brazil, India, Mexico, and Venezuela; cement and related manufacturing companies in Greece, Iran, Peru, and Mexico; textile firms in Colombia, Ecuador, Ethiopia, and Pakistan; and fertilizer companies in Greece, Peru, and Tunisia. However, IFC has begun to diversify from investments in industrial and mining companies. Some of these investments have been: a grain storage company in Colombia, as well as a hotel in Kenya, and an electric power company and a telephone company in other areas.[23] Finally, IFC has made large commitments in private development finance companies.

The Corporation has invested over $173 million in total and its investments have averaged between $1-2 million each. Generally, no investment of less than $100,000 is considered and the largest commitment during IFC's first decade of operations has been approximately $6 million. The new authority enabling IFC to borrow from the World Bank will enable the institution to consider single investments which may require commitments of $15-20 million each.

UNDERWRITING, STANDBYS, AND SALES OF INVESTMENTS BY IFC

New entrepreneurial ventures in underdeveloped countries are fraught with many problems. One of the major problems is the near nonexistence in most of these countries of a viable, adequate capital market. Equity funds are not sufficiently available for new business ventures because investors who do have capital are unwilling to incur the risks prevalent in such projects. Investment banking institutions generally have not been established in these areas.

One important function of an investment bank
is the underwriting of securities issued by business enterprises. The IFC has been performing
this function in addition to its own investment
operations. IFC generally attempts to mobilize
present local financial sources. The present trend
is for IFC to invest in new projects or expansions
of existing enterprises which are, at least, partially owned by local investors. IFC attempts by a
number of methods to encourage local participation
in the investment proposals which the institution
considers. One principal means available to IFC
which is quite effective in encouraging such local
investment is its underwriting and standby operations.

IFC's underwriting greatly assists investment
in these projects because it places the authority,
stamp of approval, guarantee, and resources of an
international financial institution behind them.
This underwriting of securities not only encourages
local investors to participate but also has facilitated the participation of European commercial
banks such as Deutsche and Dresdner Banks of Germany, Banca Commerciale Italiana of Italy, The
Banque Nationale pour le Commerce et l'Industrie
of Paris, and The Chartered Bank of London, as
well as American financial institutions such as
Kuhn, Loeb & Company, Morgan Guaranty Trust Company
of New York, Lehman Brothers, and Chase Manhattan
Bank.

As of June 30, 1966, IFC's underwriting activities totaled $25.1 million in eleven companies
located in ten countries. As of that date, approximately 70 per cent of this total had been subscribed
to by other investors.[24] In June, 1962, IFC under-
took its first underwriting commitment. With
Credito Bursatil, S.A., a Mexican investment bank,
IFC formed a syndicate for the purpose of underwriting new shares issued by Compania Fundidora de
Fierro y Acero de Monterrey, S.A. (Fundidora),
Mexico's largest privately-owned steel company.
IFC underwrote shares valued at $2,942,500.[25] This
investment will be discussed in more detail in
Chapter 5.

In addition to underwriting of public offerings
of securities, the IFC, as previously mentioned,
sells investments from its portfolio to other private investors. Some of these securities are ear-
marked for purchase only by local investors and, in
other cases, commercial and investment banks in the
capital exporting countries and development finance
companies in the less developed nations participate
by purchasing debt obligations or equities held by
IFC. The nearly $35 million of these sales of IFC
investments have not only enabled the institution
to revolve its funds, but have also facilitated one
of the Corporation's objectives of stimulating the
flow of private capital from developed to less
developed nations.

IFC AND PRIVATE DEVELOPMENT FINANCE COMPANIES

In most countries, three major obstacles hinder
efficient industrialization. First, a shortage of
investment capital exists. Second, a tool is
missing for channeling existent small savings into
feasible projects. Third, entrepreneurs who are
willing to accept risk are in short supply.[26]
Specialized financial intermediary institutions are
necessary for mobilizing capital resources and
technical know-how into the productive sector in
the process of industrialization in order to overcome these obstacles. Most countries have established such institutions commonly referred to as
"development banks." These institutions have the
primary purposes of furnishing medium- and long-
term capital funds for productive projects and the
technical advice necessary to the success of such
projects. These financial institutions may be
privately-owned, government-owned, or joint public-
private enterprises. They may invest in either the
private or public area or in both. Specific development banks may finance only projects in a single
business area, such as manufacturing, mining, agriculture, forestry, or the like.

One such type of development bank is the private development finance company. Predominantly

privately owned--a small government participation
may be necessary to initiate such an institution--
these finance companies mobilize and channel private savings into productive investments. Such in-
termediaries may channel foreign and international
investment into local projects which could not
otherwise obtain such capital themselves.

Development finance companies should have
available the following resources which facilitate
their objectives:

1. a supply of long-term capital;

2. management experienced in modern investment techniques and with a knowledge
of international and national economic
conditions;

3. contacts with foreign private business
and financial institutions and public
international financial and technical
assistance institutions.[27]

Objectives of Private Development
Finance Companies

A private development finance company must
formulate its investment policies so as to fulfill
a double role, that of being a development institution while at the same time, being a profit-making
enterprise. Therefore, a working relationship between private development finance companies and
international agencies such as those in the World
Bank Group is essential to provide an additional
source of funds, know-how, and technical services.

The finance company's operational risk incurred in performing its double role is lessened by
diversifying its portfolio. This may be done by
investing in a broad range of projects which have a
wide geographical distribution and in which the investments are balanced between equity commitments
and debt obligations.[28] Most of these companies

will not invest more than half the necessary funds
in any project. In short, the private development
finance company should operate in a manner similar
to the IFC except that it should operate in only
one country. Its management should encourage local
investors to participate in its ownership. The
ownership should be as broadly based as possible to
avert control by a narrow interest and to give the
institution a national flavor. It should underwrite security issues and be ready to sell securities from its own portfolio. And it should offer
miscellaneous services such as project feasibility
studies, economic surveys, and other consultative
operations.

The private development finance companies (DFC's)
are dissimilar to IFC in a few major aspects of
their operations and it is these dissimilarities
which have caused these institutions to fall short
of expectations of IFC officials. The DFC's are
principally lending institutions. They seldom, if
ever, take equity positions in the companies which
are their clients. In addition, they do not have
sufficient organizational capacity and bring in
outside partners only when they lack the necessary
capital. The DFC's also primarily dispense public
funds. Their share capital is relatively small and
they do not generally acquire private funds for reinvestment purposes. BANDESCO, a Spanish DFC, is
one of the few such institutions which funnel private funds into private enterprise projects.
BANDESCO accomplishes this by acquiring the bulk of
its funds from debenture issues. These debentures
are guaranteed by the credit of the large Spanish
banks.

Among these important miscellaneous services
are technical and managerial assistance, promotional
activities, and assistance to the development of
local capital markets. A private development finance company can bring in technical experts from
other countries to advise its clients and it may
place a representative on the board of the client
to assist in managerial affairs.

The development finance company may engage in
a number of promotional activities in its country.
Among these are the following:

1. arranging for general industrial
surveys and feasibility studies for
special projects;

2. formulating specific proposals for
new enterprises;

3. assisting in finding technical and
entrepreneurial partners for local
clients or for foreign investors;

4. investing in share capital and
underwriting securities, in order to
attract other investors;

5. arranging mergers, in order to
create more economic industrial units;

6. developing a capital market by
trying to broaden ownership and by
other devices; and

7. encouraging the acceptance of new
ideas in the economic sector.[29]

As a promoter, a development finance company
performs a four-step procedure. It will identify
a project that appears to be a profitable venture.
The finance company will then formulate the project by means of feasibility studies. The project
is then initiated and the development finance company will consult the services of technical experts, will plan the distribution system, and draft
the project's plant blueprints and capital structure. Finally, the project is executed. This step
involves financing, acquiring real estate, closing
contracts, and placing orders for machinery and
equipment.[30] The important element of this procedure, and the one which may insure success of the
venture, is the development finance company's function of making contact between an idea for a pro-

ject on the one hand and entrepreneurial assistance
on the other.[31]

The third principal function of a development
finance company is the development of a workable
capital market in its own region or country.[32]
The development finance company may achieve success
in this activity by a number of methods. First, it
may assist in creating a much wider distribution of
securities ownership by local investors. Secondly,
it may assist the government in establishing sound
monetary and fiscal policies so that local investors will have more confidence in the local economy.
Thirdly, it may encourage cooperation between the
public and private sectors. Finally, the development finance company should assist in maintaining a
stable market for securities.

The development finance company may implement
these objectives by a number of methods. It may
market its own shares and debentures. It may
assist in upgrading business practices. It may
initiate a securities exchange. It may help expand
the number and varieties of securities available
for investors. It may widen the securities market
by underwriting activities, assisting in public
issues of other companies' securities, initiating
mutual funds, selling from its own portfolio, and
encouraging companies to report more adequate and
meaningful financial information, resort to higher
accounting standards, implement more ethical business practices, and develop more modern financial
policies.

World Bank Group Assistance
to Private Development Finance Companies

The World Bank initiated investment activities
with private development finance companies. By the
end of the 1950's, IBRD had made loans totaling
$76.7 million to six of these companies in Austria,
Ethiopia, India, Iran, Pakistan, and Turkey, and by
the beginning of 1963, the World Bank and IFC had
invested in five more financing institutions and

total commitments from the World Bank Group amounted
to $167.1 million.[33]

In 1961, IFC took the initiative in considering
proposals for financial and technical aid to private
industrial development banks by the World Bank Group.
A Development Bank Services Department was established to coordinate these activities. In August,
1961, IFC made its first direct investment in a
private development finance company. Commitments
of $2 million were made to each of two such insti-
tutions located in Colombia, the Corporación Financiera Colombiana de Desarrollo Industrial in Bogota
and the Corporación Financiera Nacional in Medellin.
Both of these companies had been established in
1958 and 1959 respectively by Colombian banks, insurance companies, business firms, and individual
investors. The investments were made in the form
of notes fully convertible into common stock. IFC,
during the fiscal year of 1961-1962, converted
nearly $1.5 million of the $4 million total investments into common stock of the respective financing
companies. This resulted in the first holding of
common stock by IFC since the change in the Articles
permitting such action had become effective.[34] The
entire $4 million has been converted into common
stock since the commitment.

Subsequently, the World Bank and IFC began to
combine their efforts in financing the establishment
or expansion of private development finance companies. During the 1962-1963 fiscal year, the
first such combined efforts of the two institutions
took place when commitments were made in the Banque
Nationale pour le Développement Economique of
Morocco (BNDE), a development bank already established by the Moroccan government and owned jointly
by American, Belgian, French, German, and Italian
banks, as well as by the Moroccan government. The
government held a majority position in the company.
In order to qualify for World Bank Group assistance,
no finance company may have its ownership controlled
by the government. Therefore, a new issue of ten
million shares was made. IFC subscribed to shares
amounting to approximately $1.5 million. Thus, the

government interest was reduced to a minority position. The World Bank also made a loan at that time
to the bank.[35]

Another example of joint World Bank-IFC cooperation resulted in the financing of a development finance company in the Philippines during the
1962-1963 fiscal year. Through IFC-Filipino efforts, the Private Development Corporation of the
Philippines (PDCP) was established. A World Bank
loan of $15 million was supplemented with a standby
commitment by IFC covering $4.4 million of capital
shares out of $6.4 million offered. IFC, after
encouraging a number of significant international
financial institutions to participate in the equity
issue, eventually invested about $205,000. Alto-
gether, eighteen private investment firms and banks
purchased 30 per cent of PDCP's shares. These included fourteen American institutions as well as
two British, one German, and one Japanese.[36] Included among these financial institutions were
Continental International Finance Corporation, a
subsidiary of Continental Illinois National Bank of
Chicago; The American Express Company; The Bank of
Tokyo; Deutsche Bank A.G.; Lehman Brothers; Manufacturers Hanover International Finance Corporation;
New York Hanseatic Corporation; and Wells Fargo
Bank International Corporation.[37]

Heavy commitments by IFC to private development finance companies continued during 1963-1964.
Investments in common stock were made in companies
which also received loans from the World Bank.
These included the Finnish Industrialization Fund,
the Malaysian Industrial Development Finance
Limited, and the Industrial Finance Corporation of
Thailand. IFC also invested in shares of the Industrial Development Bank of Turkey, already a recipient of loans from the World Bank and credits
from the International Development Association (IDA),
and in other finance companies in Colombia, Nigeria,
and Venezuela.[38] Thus, the tendency seemed to be
for IFC to subscribe to and purchase or underwrite
shares in these institutions whereas the World Bank
and IDA would commit loan funds to them.

Financing of private development finance companies by the World Bank Group, as of March 31, 1967, has been fairly extensive. According to the data shown in Table 2, World Bank financing of twenty-five such institutions has amounted to $570.6 million. The financial resources available to these development finance companies was slightly over one billion dollars and share capital amounted to approximately $270 million. Nearly 75 per cent of this capital was provided by local investors while foreign investors--mainly financial institutions in the United States, Europe, and Japan-- have invested about $53 million and IFC commitments have totaled $14.1 million. In addition, these finance companies have been able to raise loan funds from many sources including $477.7 million from the World Bank and IDA. Furthermore, long-term, low interest loans have often been granted by the host governments to some of these institutions. Thus, these private development finance companies have been able to undertake investments in industrial enterprises totaling nearly $1.5 billion.[39]

The IFC has assisted development finance companies in a number of ways. Besides assisting in financing, IFC helps train the staff of these special banks, assists them in project analyses and evaluations, is represented on the boards of some of them, and participates with them, in some cases, in jointly financing industrial projects. IFC will accept a position on the board of only private development finance companies. Its policy is not to be a member of the board of an industrial company. Also IFC refers investments to these institutions when the total of funds to be committed is below IFC's minimum criterion. A list of IFC investments in privately-owned development finance companies is presented in Table 3.

In summary, IFC has assisted in industrial development and the strengthening of local capital markets by its investments in these institutions. Means for channeling foreign and domestic capital into small and medium sized projects have been

established by World Bank Group activity in this
financial area.   The equity investments and underwriting by IFC have helped to improve the capital
markets in the less developed countries in which
these development agencies are located.

MISCELLANEOUS OPERATIONS

In addition to its industrial development financing, underwriting and standby agreements, and
private development finance company operations, IFC
performs other miscellaneous but related activities.
In conjunction with its investments, IFC acts as a
promoter in encouraging local and foreign capital
to participate in a project.   Market and geographical surveys may be drafted with IFC's assistance.

Because of several years' experience in industrial development financing, IFC has assumed responsibility within the World Bank Group for certain
activities, among them the previously analyzed
financing of private development finance companies.
Another function over which IFC has been given
major responsibility is that of technical and financial appraisal of all investment proposals for
industrial and mining projects which are submitted
to the three institutions constituting the World
Bank Group.   This responsibility was assumed by IFC
in 1965.   In general, IFC acts as a consultant not
only to the World Bank and IDA, but also to the
private development finance companies in which the
Group has invested.

Table 2

Financing of Private Development Finance Companies (DFC's)
by the World Bank Group
(As of March 31, 1967)

Company	Type of Group Activity	Group Financing $ million	DFC Total Re-sources $ mil-lion – 1/1/67
Austria			
Osterreichische Investitions-kredit A.G. (IVK)	3 Bank loans	23.3	57.8
China (Taiwan)			
China Development Corporation (CDC)	1 IDA Credit & 1 Bank loan	19.9	37.4
Colombia			
Corporación Financiera Colombiana (CFC) Corporación Financiera Nacional (CFN) Corporación Financiera de Caldas Corporación Financiera del Valle Corporación Financiera del Norte	3 IFC invest-ments & 1 Bank loan	29.8	85.1
Ethiopia			
Development Bank of Ethiopia (DBE)	2 Bank loans	4.0	7.7

Finland			
The Industrialization Fund of Finland (IFF)	2 Bank loans & 1 IFC investment	21.3	24.2
Greece			
National Investment Bank for Industrial Development, S.A. (NIBID)	1 IFC investment	0.7	15.6
India			
Industrial Credit and Investment Corporation of India, Ltd. (ICICI)	6 Bank loans	139.1	132.3
Iran			
Industrial and Mining Development Bank of Iran (IMDBI)	3 Bank loans	40.1	62.2
Israel			
Industrial Development Bank of Israel (IDBI)	1 Bank loan	20.1	223.5
Ivory Coast			
Banque Ivoirienne de Développement Industriel, S.A. (BIDI)	1 IFC investment	0.2	8.0
Liberia			
Liberian Bank for Industrial Development and Investment (LBIDI)	1 IFC investment	0.2	2.1

(continued)

53

Table 2 (Continued)

Company	Type of Group Activity	Group Financing $ million	DFC Total Re-sources $ million - 1/1/67
Malaysia			
Malaysian Industrial Development Finance Limited (MIDFL)	1 Bank loan & 1 IFC investment	9.3	25.9
Morocco			
Banque Nationale pour le Développement Economique (BNDE)	2 Bank loans & 1 IFC investment	34.0	31.9
Nigeria			
Nigerian Industrial Development Bank (NIDB)	1 IFC investment	1.4	15.7
Pakistan			
Pakistan Industrial Credit and Investment Corp. Ltd. (PICIC)	6 Bank loans & 1 IFC investment	109.3	118.8
Philippines			
Private Development Corporation of the Philippines (PDCP)	2 Bank loans & 1 IFC investment	44.4	23.6
Spain			
Banco del Desarrollo Economico Español, S.A. (BANDESCO)	2 IFC investments	0.6	63.3

Thailand			
Industrial Finance Corporation of Thailand (IFCT)	1 Bank loan & 1 IFC investment	2.7	6.4
Tunisia			
Société Nationale d'Investissement (SNI)	1 Bank loan & 1 IFC investment	5.6	9.6
Turkey			
Industrial Development Bank of Turkey (IDB)	3 Bank loans, 1 IFC investment, & 4 IDA credits	63.5	82.9
Venezuela			
C.A. Venezolana de Desarrollo (CAVENDES)	1 IFC investment	1.3	14.7
Totals		$570.8	$1,048.7

Source: The United Nations & the Business World (New York: Business International, 1967), pp. 77-78.

55

Table 3

Investments by International Finance Corporation in Private Development Finance Companies (1961-1966)

Country and Institution	Operational Investment
Colombia	
Corporación Financiera Colombiana	$ 2,023,730
Corporación Financiera Nacional	2,042,000
Corporación Financiera de Caldas	701,403
Finland	
Industrialization Fund of Finland	158,644
Greece	
National Investment Bank for Industrial Development, S.A.	719,082
Ivory Coast	
Banque Ivoirienne de Développement Industriel, S.A.	204,081
Liberia	
Liberian Bank for Industrial Development and Investment (Standby/underwriting $250,000)	---
Malaysia	
Malaysian Industrial Development Finance, Ltd. (also underwriting $490,000)	817,917
Morocco	
Banque Nationale pour le Développement Economique	1,495,774

Country and Institution	Operational Investment
Nigeria	
Nigerian Industrial Development Bank, Ltd. (underwriting $1,400,000)	---
Pakistan	
Pakistan Industrial Credit and Investment Corporation, Ltd.	440,000
Philippines	
Private Development Corporation of the Philippines (underwriting $4,359,063)	---
Spain	
Banco del Desarrollo Economico Español, S.A.	585,351
Thailand	
Industrial Finance Corporation of Thailand	193,108
Tunisia	
Société Nationale d'Investissement	571,428
Turkey	
Turkiye Sinai Kalkinma Bankasi, A.S.	916,667
Venezuela	
C.A. Venezolana de Desarrollo (Sociedad Financiera)	1,336,183
Total Operational Investments	$ 12,205,368
Total Standby and Underwriting	6,499,063

Source: IFC, Annual Report, 1965-1966 (Washington, D.C.: International Finance Corporation, 1966), Appendix C.

CHAPTER **4** PROJECT
EVALUATION
METHODOLOGY

INITIATION OF A PROJECT STUDY

A potential investment project in a developing
country becomes known to IFC by a number of means.
A new or an expanding enterprise may apply directly
to IFC or the World Bank for assistance--stating in
the preliminary contact that local capital is unavailable. A local financial institution may
notify IFC that a promising investment should be
investigated. An example of this method occurred
in 1965 when the Pakistan Industrial Credit and
Investment Corporation (PICIC) informed IFC of the
expansion plans of Packages Limited, a successful
packaging materials producer. IFC's follow-up
resulted in an operational investment in Packages
of $3,151,662. This case is discussed in Chapter 6.

Another method sometimes employed by financial
institutions to assist new enterprises is industrial promotion by the institution itself. The
institution is limited by the frequent costliness
of promotion and the uncertainty of immediate
return or any return at all. In an address by
Martin M. Rosen, Executive Vice President of IFC,
he stated that "projects which simply walk in the
front door and present themselves across the
counter are usually rather shopworn and not particularly attractive."[1] He believes that an organization such as IFC should promote new enterprises
in developing countries but that top management
should control such activity closely.

58

An investment proposal to be considered by IFC may arise from any, or a combination, of these methods. Regardless of the way in which IFC is informed about the enterprise, if the firm wishes an IFC investment commitment, an application for funds must be made. This application must contain preliminary information which would usually be requested by any other financial investment institution. This information required to be set forth in the application is presented in Table 4.

IFC PROJECT EVALUATION PROCEDURE

The application with the information shown in Table 4, as requested by IFC, may be submitted by a businessman, a group of businessmen, or the company officials themselves. The application is then given to an IFC investment officer.[2] IFC employs several investment officers who specialize in a geographical region. The investment officer in whose region the proposed project is located will be assigned to study the application and accompanying papers.

The investment officer and a committee of colleagues, after studying the application, will decide whether or not IFC should accept the project and whether further study should be made. The investment officer and executive officers of IFC may, and in most cases do, travel to the project site for personal observation and investigation. If, after this observation period, the investment officers have decided the investment should be made by IFC, a report advising acceptance is made to the executive officers of IFC. The final decision is made at this level.

In a few cases, the decision may be made in a more informal manner. The investment may be approved and papers signed and executed by investment officers while present at the project site. In 1966, IFC committed funds to the expansion of a cement plant in Malaysia.[3] Mr. Judhvir Parmar, an IFC investment officer, studied the application and

Table 4

Information Requested by IFC
in an Investment Proposal Application

1. The purpose of the proposed financing;

2. A brief description of new construction or machinery to be purchased;

3. The amount, source, and type of
   capital available or promised as
   well as capital to be raised locally
   or abroad;

4. A description of the company;

5. Names, financial condition, and
   biographical sketches of principal
   shareowners, directors, and
   management personnel;

6. Description of present and proposed
   company productive facilities;

7. A review of the company operations
   including products, markets, labor,
   and competition;

8. An analysis of all tariffs, import
   quotas, tax exemptions, other market
   restrictions, and other laws which
   affect, or might affect, company
   operations;

9. Copies of annual reports and auditors'
   reports, if available, including
   balance sheets, income statements,
   and other financial statements, for
   the last five years as well as income
   tax returns and statements to shareowners;

10. Copies of special laws or regulations applicable to the company;

11. Copies of recent prospectuses or valuations;

12. Copies of the charter, by-laws, or articles of association, if available;

13. Copies of loan contracts, options on shares, patent licenses, pending claims, or other information material to a present or potential shareowner, if in existence;

14. Financial forecasts for the first five years after the proposed financing is completed;

15. Company studies of engineering costs, market surveys, or other such research;

16. Details of arrangements with consultants;

17. A statement showing what party is furnishing the information about the company to be financed;

18. Bank or other relevant references;

19. Any other relevant miscellaneous information about the applicant or the proposed project.

Source: "General Policies," (Washington, D.C.: International Finance Corporation, March, 1964), pp. 7-9.

visited the company. While there, Mr. Parmar was
joined by a ranking IFC officer who had been in
Asia investigating another proposal and the decision was made to commit IFC at that time. The
papers were signed and executed without their for-
mal presentation to IFC directors. In this case,
the company had demonstrated a good past record,
management was excellent, and rapid expansion of
the supply of cement in Malaysia was required.
Thus a decision to commit IFC funds was feasible
and was subsequently approved by IFC officials in
Washington.

All negotiations before and after approval of
an IFC investment are kept in the strictest confidence by IFC. The dealings are financial in
nature and the applicant is a private enterprise.
Thus, the traditional nondisclosure of financial
information is practiced. If the investment proposal is approved by IFC, the latter will issue a
press release informing the public about the general details of the commitment.

CRITERIA FOR PROJECT APPROVAL

Before IFC will approve a project application,
the company or its sponsors must demonstrate to IFC
that the project is sound in three ways. The project must be economically, technically, and finan-
cially feasible. These are the criteria, therefore,
which IFC uses in its study of the project according to the procedure discussed in the preceding
section.

First, the project must be economically feasible. Accepted standards are being established
in less developed countries (LDC's) for the most
economic minimum capacity for certain installations.
For example, the present minimum daily capacity for
an ammonia plant in an LDC is 600 tons; for a paper
mill, 40-50 tons; for a cement plant, 100 tons.
Before economies of scale are possible, these
standard minimum capacities are necessary. Excep-
tions to the established norms do exist. A steel

mill with an annual capacity of 200,000 tons is
being built in Malaysia. Normally, steel mills
should produce at least 1 million tons annually.
However, this plant will be more profitable at a
lower output because charcoal will be used as a
reducing agent. Charcoal actually makes a better
reducing agent than does coke and it is a normal
by-product from waste rubber trees in Malaysia.[4]

Another example of the necessity for economic
feasibility is a textile mill. Another textile
mill added to the hundreds existing in India or
Pakistan would not be practical nor would the estab-
listment of a textile mill in some Central African
nations be feasible because these economies might
not be able to support even one mill.[5]

The second feasibility criterion concerns the
technical characteristics of the project. The project must not only benefit the local economy but
it must have available the necessary labor skills
and raw materials. Managerial skills must either
exist, or they must be imported[6] as was necessary
in the cases of Arewa Textiles Ltd. of Nigeria and
NPK-Engrais S.A.T. of Tunisia. Japanese interests
organized and trained personnel in the Arewa case
and Swedish interests developed the NPK-Engrais
management. Both projects received IFC assistance
and are analyzed in subsequent chapters of this
study.

In addition to surveying managerial, labor,
and raw material needs, the market for the project's product(s) must be analyzed. A local market
must exist for the output. Mr. James S. Raj, IFC
Vice President, stated that IFC now demands a very
rigorous market analysis because of lessons learned
from earlier experience where sales less than those
forecast had resulted in lowered profits for companies in which IFC had invested.[7]

Thirdly, the applicant seeking an IFC commitment must demonstrate that the project is finan-
cially feasible. The financial plan must be
realistic in terms of available sources of financing.
Provision for such contingencies as cost overruns

must be considered.[8] Profitability forecasts and
budgeting systems should be sound.

During these feasibility studies, IFC may suggest certain changes which result in improved applications. Such a case in point occurred during IFC's
eighth fiscal year, 1963-1964, when IFC invested in
Industria del Hierro, S.A., a Mexican heavy equipment manufacturer. Before completion of financing
of this company, a revised financial plan was
drafted and approved enabling the company to finance
a broader product line, to combine managerial and
technical functions more closely, and to establish
better financial and corporation relationships
between the parent company and its subsidiaries.[9]

Finally, after the project has been analyzed
for its economic, technical, and financial feasibility, its sponsors must demonstrate to IFC that sufficient funds on reasonable terms are unavailable
from private sources. What constitutes the diligent
search for funds required by IFC differs from project
to project. For example, if the project's sponsors
have approached the major financial institutions
which are strongest in the area and have been turned
away, this may be all that is necessary. Such a case
could be Barclays of London in the case of a project
located in Africa. Also, the funds may be available
but a long period of time may elapse before they are
obtainable and, thus, the entrepreneurial push in the
project may lose momentum. Local banks may require
tying arrangements which would be too binding. Thus,
in one case, sponsors may seek out local and international funds from many sources whereas another set
of sponsors may inquire at only one or two banks, and
IFC will be satisfied that in both cases a diligent
search was made.[10] In some cases, IFC fills a gap
where the project's total needs are not satisfied.
In other cases, IFC will initiate the investment
process as a last resort to encourage other investors to act. This was true in the case of Fábrica
Española Magnetos, S.A., a Spanish manufacturer of
automotive electrical equipment. No other funds
would have been committed had IFC not agreed to invest in the company. This case is analyzed in
Chapter 8.

When the feasibility studies have been completed, IFC has examined the application and has
been satisfied that the project is sound in all
these aspects, and the funding has been arranged,
IFC's top officers will then vote to commit funds
as discussed in the previous section. For every
project approved for IFC investment, a number are
turned down. One estimate is that four or five
projects are refused for every one accepted.[11]
During the second half of IFC's second fiscal year,
1957/1958, 235 proposals were received. About 40
per cent of these were not within the requirements
of the policies and charter of IFC. For example,
some were located in nonmember countries, some were
for straight loans or export financing, and some
were applications for funds in an amount lower than
IFC's operating standards required.[12] Of the remaining proposals, some were in a stage too early
for consideration, some offered insufficient information; others were not approved because they were
not feasible economically, technically, or finan-
cially, or their sponsors were inexperienced, or
their economic value to their country of location
was unproven. Thus, only fifteen to twenty projects
from the original 235 proved promising for IFC ·
action during the near-term after June 30, 1958.[13]
This presents an example of the diligent study made
in IFC's evaluation procedure in order to satisfy
the feasibility criteria heretofore discussed. And
it is still possible for problems to arise after
IFC has made a commitment as some of the case
studies in subsequent chapters will demonstrate.

ACCOUNTING AND FINANCIAL REPORTING
AFTER PROJECT APPROVAL

After IFC has approved the project financing
and committed the funds, certain accounting and
financial reporting procedures must be followed by
the recipient firm as long as the investment agreement is in force between IFC and the enterprise.
Certain financial statements and information must
be submitted by the company. Specific public
accounting standards must be practiced in reporting

financial information. Some of the financial statements must be audited by independent public account-
ants with specific prescribed qualifications, and
these audits must be performed according to accepted
standards and procedures. The following sections
will elaborate upon these requirements.

Financial Statements[14]

In addition to the basic financial statements
and related company information, IFC requires an
annual balance sheet and income and surplus statements for each year during which the investment is
in effect. These statements should show comparative figures for the previous year and should be
audited. Quarterly balance sheets and surplus and
income statements showing comparative figures for
the corresponding period of the previous year are
also required. However, an audit of the quarterly
statements is not required.

Income statements should show principal items
separately. Such items as net sales, cost of goods
sold, expenses--selling, administrative, and general net operating profit, nonoperating income and/or
expenses, income taxes, and net income after taxes--
should be included although the income statement
is not limited to these items. Ratio statements
are recommended. These are statements which show
each item as a percentage of net sales.

Other information required pertains to statements which elaborate upon significant operating
information and give details about nonrecurring
income and expenses or extraordinary items. Statements should be provided showing operating costs,
income, and expenses where these items are relevant
to the quantity of a material produced. This requirement pertains to mining and petroleum firms
where depletion of mineral resources is important.
A company with subsidiaries should either submit
consolidated financial statements or data which
specifically refers to the subsidiaries in addition
to the firm's own statements.

Public Accounting Standards[15]

IFC requires that generally accepted accounting principles be recognized when financial statements of its clients are constructed. No attempt is made to prescribe specific principles to be followed but this responsibility is delegated by IFC to the accounting profession. Accounting principles, however, do vary from country to country, and, therefore, IFC requires that the accounting principles adhered to in a certain country have some support in practice as well as in theory and that they are used in preparing statements for shareowners, lenders, and other interested parties.

Any differences between statements being presented and those conforming to statutory requirements must be disclosed to IFC. For instance, some countries allow assets to be understated and liabilities to be overstated as long as some system is used. In some countries, property may be carried on the books at replacement cost or some value other than historical cost less depreciation. Some countries allow certain gains and losses to be excluded from the income statement. Among these items may be profits on sale of property, bonuses paid to directors, and income taxes. Foreign exchange losses are handled differently in various countries. If the practices in reporting are generally accepted locally, they may be used in reporting to IFC. However, full diclosure must be made of the effects such practices will have on financial and operating results. Finally, if conversion of one currency into another is necessary, the conversion method and rates utilized must be disclosed.

The independent public accountant or accounting firm handling the audit must be in good standing and entitled to practice in its domicile. The accountant or his firm may not have had any financial interest in the audited company nor should the accountant have been connected in any official manner such as director or officer of the firm during the period covered by the report.

Auditing Standards and Procedures[16]

The annual audit must be sufficient in depth and detail to allow the auditor to express an opinion that the financial statements present a fair and accurate picture of the operations of the company during the reporting period. The auditor must confirm accounts and notes receivable by contacting debtors of the subject company and must witness the physical inventory taking if the amounts of these assets are material. Certain forms are prescribed by IFC for the auditor's report. A short-form contains a discussion of the basic financial information and a long-form contains a discussion in detail of the items in the short-form. These forms contain the auditor's opinion about the financial condition of the company.

CONCLUSIONS AND SPECIFIC CASES

Two operations of IFC have been discussed in this chapter. The first was the evaluation of projects before they have been accepted and the second was the control exercised by IFC over the recipient enterprise after an investment commitment has been made. Some conclusions have been drawn on the basis of some cases of IFC investments. These will be discussed in this concluding section.

Appraisal of four areas are made during the evaluation of a project. These are the economic, technical, managerial, and financial aspects of the enterprise. Significant revisions in the cost of a project may result from the evaluation of a project by IFC. In some cases, superfluous construction may be avoided. An example of this occurred when the Pakistan government commissioned a study of the cement industry in that country. Government consultants recommended expansion of two existing plants and construction of three additional plants. The Pakistan Industrial Credit and Investment Corporation (PICIC) sought assistance from IFC and foreign investors and the result was a commitment

by IFC to assist the expansion of the Ismail Cement
Industries Limited. This investment is discussed
in Chapter 6. IFC commissioned a new survey of the
industry. The second survey revealed that the
first study was too optimistic and overcapacity was
avoided as the Pakistan government was persuaded by
IFC to reduce its expansion program.[17]

In some cases, the cost of a project is underestimated. The cost of the 1965 expansion of
Packages, Limited, a packaging materials manufacturer located in West Pakistan, assisted by an IFC
commitment, was approximately 35 per cent above the
estimated cost at the time of application to IFC
for assistance. This project is also discussed in
Chapter 6.

Another project whose proposal was modified by
IFC's evaluation was the commitment in 1962 to finance a new Tunisian company, NPK-Engrais, S.A.T.,
jointly with Aktiebolaget Forenade Superfosfat-
fabriker, a leading Swedish producer of chemical
fertilizers, and Freeport International, Inc., a
subsidiary of Freeport Sulphur Company of the United
States. This project is discussed in Chapter 7.
The IFC evaluation resulted in improving the project's marketing arrangements, adding a sulphuric
acid plant to increase the project's profitability,
and the encouraging of an additional technical
partner to participate in the joint venture.[18]

The reporting standards which IFC has formulated, as described in earlier sections of this
chapter, are quite worthy in theory. However, an
analysis of the implementation of these standards
and procedures shows that they are not always followed to the letter of the provisions, especially
when shareowners are concerned. IFC reporting
regulations state that major items should be shown
separately and should include net sales, cost of
goods sold, operating expenses, etc., as a minimum
of items to be disclosed. Some annual reports of
IFC-financed firms reveal these items and their
amounts. Some do not. Although local accounting
standards may allow the nondisclosure of some of

the pertinent items in financial statements, nearly
all companies assisted by IFC are held by a number
of shareowners. IFC encourages these firms to sell
stock to the public. The reporting standards of
IFC conform fairly closely to American Securities
and Exchange Commission requirements for American
firms. Apparently IFC requires rather strict reporting standards but this does not insure that
annual reports to shareowners will reveal information as lucidly as the company reports to IFC.
An example is the annual report of Ismail Cement
Industries of West Pakistan. The "income of casual
nature"--1,341,173 rupees--is not explained. Depreciation of plant and equipment is not included
in the profit statement. These shortcomings are
disclosed in the annual report. However, the
annual report is generally vague and confusing
especially when compared with the annual report of
Packages, Ltd., a West Pakistani firm previously
mentioned. Packages' report is very revealing and
conforms very well to IFC reporting standards and
requirements.

The above pattern of revealing versus non-
revealing annual reports of IFC-assisted firms
seems to be quite prevalent. However, IFC is encouraging firms it finances to report the same information to their shareowners in the same manner
as they are required to report to IFC. In fact,
IFC's requirements for accounting standards have
led to a vast improvement in reporting by these
firms. This has led to improvement in local capital markets because these companies, by reporting
more accurately, are better able to market their
securities. Foreign financial institutions participating with IFC in financing these projects have
approved these standards although they may be located in a country whose philosophy may be to report very little financial data. The need for
uniform accounting systems in the LDC's is a major
problem.[19]

CHAPTER **5** THE INTERNATIONAL
FINANCE CORPORATION
IN LATIN AMERICA

INTRODUCTION

The geographical area in which IFC has been
most active is Latin America. Of the 124 commitments made by IFC during its first decade of
operations, 69, or 54.6 per cent, were made to
companies located in Central and South America and
the Caribbean area. During the 1956-1966 decade,
total investments by IFC amounted to $172,361,343.
Latin American companies received 58.3 per cent of
this amount, or $100,517,328. Commitments by coun-
try are shown in Table 5.

Among the reasons why IFC has been relatively
more active in Latin America is the fact that IFC's
first investment was made in 1957 to a Brazilian
company, Siemens do Brasil Companhia de Electrici-
dade, a subsidiary of Siemens of Germany. In addition, the World Bank Group has been quite active in
Latin America. By early 1966, the Bank had made
155 loans to 18 Latin American countries. These
loans amounted to almost $2.5 billion. Mexico had
received $616 million of these loans; Colombia $389
million; and Brazil $347 million.[1] Thus a great
deal of investment experience in Latin America was
inherited by IFC from the World Bank.

Since its first investment in Latin America in
1957, IFC has made 69 commitments in 13 countries
to 47 industrial firms and 4 private development

71

Table 5

IFC Investment, Standby and
Underwriting Commitments, 1956-1966,
Latin America

Country	Initial Commitment	No. of Commitments	Funds Committed
Argentina	1960	5	$ 13,710,000
Brazil	1957	8	22,483,949
Chile	1957	9	10,291,346
Colombia	1959	15	14,382,131
Costa Rica	1962	2	589,552
Ecuador	1965	1	2,000,584
El Salvador	1959	1	140,000
Guatemala	1958	1	200,000
Honduras	1964	2	377,500
Jamaica	1961	1	224,000
Mexico	1957	12	21,713,723
Peru	1959	7	8,913,290
Venezuela	1960	5	5,491,253
		69	$100,517,328

Source: IFC, Annual Report 1965-1966 (Washington,
         D.C.: International Finance Corporation,
         1966), p. 4.

finance companies. Operational investments by IFC
in this area during the 1956-1966 period have totaled $83,820,718 and underwriting and standby com-
mitments have totaled $16,696,610.[2] The 69 invest-
ments have averaged about $1.5 million each and
have been spread steadily over the 10-year period
as contrasted to accelerated activities of IFC in
Africa and Asia in recent years.

     The individual investments are shown in detail
in Table 6. Of the 47 companies listed, 13 have
been the recipient of more than one IFC investment.
The list includes 2 of only 3 investments in which
IFC has incurred losses on sales of its investments.
These were Durisol del Peru, S.A., a company estab-

lished in 1959 to produce a special lightweight
building material, and Berry, Selvey y Cia., S.A.,
a maker of home furniture. IFC made a loan of
$300,000 to Durisol at the time of its establishment.
Because of production and sales problems, the company had to close down operations in 1962. Attempts
were made by IFC and other creditors to revive the
firm but these attempts failed and the company's
assets were auctioned off. IFC was an unsecured
creditor of Durisol and, thus, lost the entire investment.[3]

   In addition to the Durisol loss, IFC has incurred problems with three other investments in
Latin America. Two of these are located in Peru
and one is in Colombia. All three companies have
incurred losses and defaulted on parts of their
debt obligations. These are FERTISA and Luren, S.A.
and Ladrillos Calcareos, S.A.--two associated companies which received jointly one IFC investment--
of Peru, and Berry, Selvey y Cia., S.A., of Colombia. The FERTISA investment will be discussed in
more detail later in this chapter. Part of the
Berry, Selvey y Cia. investment was written off
during IFC's 1964-1965 fiscal year.[4] Improvements
have been noted in the Luren-Ladrillos Calcareos
and Berry, Selvey investments since refinancing
operations have been implemented by these firms.

   IFC investments in some of the companies
listed in Table 6 have been more favorable than
those just discussed. The $3 million loan to Com-
pañia Manufacturera de Papeles y Cartónes, S.A.,
of Chile, in 1962 was the first IFC investment
made in association with a loan from the Inter-
American Development Bank. Also in that fiscal
year, IFC participated in the first sale of convertible debentures made by a Mexican company
under a new Mexican law. This was a $5 million
issue made in New York by Tubos de Acero de Mexico,
S.A., a steel tube products manufacturer in Mexico.[5]

   The remainder of this chapter contains brief
detailed analyses of selected IFC operations in
Latin America. Five investments by IFC in indus-

Table 6

IFC Commitments in Latin America by Company

Company	Country	Operational Investment	Standby and Underwriting
Acindar Industria Argentina de Aceros, S.A.	Argentina	$3,660,000	---
Papelera Rio Parana, S.A.	"	3,000,000	---
Fábrica Argentina de Engranajes, S.A.I.C.	"	1,500,000	---
PASA, Petroquimica Argentina, S.A.I.C.	"	3,050,000	---
Celulosa Argentina, S.A.	"	2,500,000	---
Siemens do Brasil Cia. de Electricidade,	Brazil	2,000,000	---
Olinkraft, S.A. Celulose e Papel	"	1,200,000	---
D.L.R. Plasticos do Brasil, S.A.	"	450,000	---
Willys-Overland do Brasil, S.A. Industria e Comercio	"	2,450,000	---
Companhia Mineira de Cimento Portland, S.A.	"	1,200,000	---
Champion Celulose, S.A.	"	4,000,000	---
Acos Villares, S.A.	"	5,051,068	---
Papel e Celulose Catarinense, S.A.	"	6,132,881	---
Empresa Minera de Mantos Blancos, S.A.	Chile	4,337,500	---
Fideos y Alimentos Carozzi, S.A.	"	1,653,846	---
Cementos Bio-Bio, S.A.	"	1,300,000	---

74

Company	Country	Operational Investment	Standby and Underwriting
Compañia Manufacturera de Papeles y Cartónes, S.A.	Chile	$3,000,000	---
Laminas del Caribe, S.A.	Colombia	500,000	---
Industrias Alimenticias Noel, S.A.	"	2,020,208	---
Envases Colombianos, S.A.	"	700,000	---
Berry, Selvey y Cia., S.A.	"	170,000	---
Electromanufacturas, S.A.	"	500,000	---
Corporación Financiera Colombiana	"	2,023,730	---
Corporación Financiera Nacional	"	2,042,000	---
Compañia Colombiana de Tejidos, S.A.	"	2,000,000	---
Corporación Financiera de Caldas	"	701,403	---
Forjas de Colombia, S.A.	"	749,628	$ 352,109
Almacenes Generales de Deposito Santa Fe, S.A. "Almaviva"	"	1,000,000	---
Industria Ganadera Colombiana, S.A.	"	1,623,053	---
Productos de Concreto, S.A.	Costa Rica	278,751	310,801

(continued)

Table 6 (Continued)

Company	Country	Operational Investment	Standby and Underwriting
La Internacional, S.A.	Ecuador	$2,000,584	---
Industrias Textiles,S.A.	El Salvador	140,000	---
Industria Harinera Guatemalteca, S.A.	Guatemala	200,000	---
Empresa de Curtidos Centro Americana, S.A.	Honduras	377,500	---
Jamaica Pre-Mix, Ltd.	Jamaica	224,000	---
Industrias Perfect Circle, S.A.	Mexico	800,000	---
Bristol de Mexico, S.A.	"	520,000	---
Acero Solar, S.A.	"	280,000	---
Compañia Fundidora de Fierro y Acero de Monterrey, S.A.	"	1,632,995	$14,769,159
Tubos de Acero de Mexico, S.A. (TAMSA)	"	250,000	750,000
Quimica del Rey, S.A.	"	750,000	---
Industria del Hierro, S.A.	"	1,961,569	---
Industrias Reunidas, S.A.	Peru	250,000	---
Luren, S.A., and Ladrillos Calcareos, S.A.	"	280,000	---
Durisol del Peru, S.A.	"	300,000	---

Company	Country	Operational Investment	Standby and Underwriting
Fertilizantes Sinteticos, S.A. (FERTISA)	Peru	$4,083,290	---
Cemento Andino, S.A.	"	2,400,000	---
Compañia de Cemento Pacasmayo, S.A.	"	1,600,000	---
Siderurgica Venezolana "Sivensa," S.A.	Venezuela	3,140,529	---
Diablitos Venezolanos, C.A.	"	500,000	---
C.A. Venezolana de Desarrollo (Sociedad Financiera)	"	1,336,183	---
Dominguez y Cia.- Caracas, S.A.	"	---	$ 514,541
Totals		$83,820,718	$16,696,610

Source: IFC, Annual Report 1965-1966 (Washington,
          D.C.: International Finance Corporation,
          1966), Appendix C. pp. 32, 34, 36, and 38.

77

trial companies and all four commitments made to
private development finance companies in the area
will be covered. The industrial companies are
Fertilizantes Sinteticos, S.A. (FERTISA) in Peru;
PASA, Petroquimica Argentina, S.A.I.C., of Argentina; Compañia Fundidora de Fierro y Acero de Monterrey, S.A. (Fundidora) of Mexico; and Acos Villares, S.A., and Papel e Celulose Catarinense, S.A.,
both of Brazil.

These companies were selected for a number of
reasons. FERTISA has been a troublesome investment
because of a partial default in repayments of loans
made to the company. PASA is a joint international
business venture which has brought a number of foreign financial interests together to finance a project needed by Argentina. The Fundidora investment
was a major underwriting operation by IFC and has
resulted in expanding one of the strongest companies
in Latin America. The two Brazilian companies are
covered because of the relative size of the IFC investments and because of the products manufactured.

FERTILIZANTES SINTETICOS S.A. (FERTISA)

The Republic of Peru, a country with an area
of 496,222 square miles and a population of over
12 million, extends along the west coast of South
America and is the third largest nation on the continent. It is bordered on the north by Ecuador and
Colombia, on the east by Bolivia and Brazil, on the
south by Chile, and on the west by the Pacific
Ocean. It is a land of rain forests, a mountainous
border and desert areas. The population is 46 per
cent Indian, 43 per cent mestizo or of mixed race,
and 11 per cent white.

Peru's economy is based on agriculture. This
sector contributes 25 per cent of the nation's
gross national product and half the people depend
on agriculture for a living. Peru is also the
world's largest producer and exporter of fish meal.
Mining is very important and contributes 16 per
cent to GNP, as does the industrial sector.   Other

significant exports are metals, cotton, sugar, coffee, and wool. Copper is the nation's third most valuable export.[6]

Rapid industrialization of urban areas has resulted in lowered industrial productivity because of a shortage of skilled labor, insufficient technical training, poor housing, inadequate food, and disease. These problems have all arisen because of the great influx of population into the cities.

The shortage of food in Peru has been recognized by the World Bank Group and, as a result, the World Bank has been relatively active in lending to Peru. The agricultural sector has been the recipient of many of these loans. Loans have been made for highways to facilitate the exportation of rubber, cocoa, bananas, and timber found in the Andes. Irrigation resulting from World Bank investment has opened up new land in northern Peru for the growing of crops such as corn.

One of the earliest IFC investments was made in Peru in 1959. Among the basic ingredients for increasing agricultural production is fertilizer. In 1959, a new company, Fertilizantes Sinteticos S.A. (FERTISA) was formed in Callao, a city just north of Lima. The company was established to operate a plant for the production of synthetic ammonia and its derivatives, including ammonium nitrate and sulfate fertilizers. Among the company's other products are liquid oxygen, nitric acid, and aqueous ammonia solution.

The principal sponsor of the project was Montecatini-Edison Chemical Company of Milan, Italy. Among other shareholders of FERTISA, besides well-known Peruvian business and agricultural groups and individuals, were a number of foreign financial institutions. Among these was Handelsfinanz A.G. of Zurich. Shareholders of Handelsfinanz include Banca Commerciale Italiana of Milan, Union de Banque Suisses of Zurich, Credit Suisse of Zurich, Hambros Bank of London, Ltd., de Rothschild Frères of Paris, and First Boston Corporation of New York.[7] Peruvians hold a majority of the shares of FERTISA.

Original production capacity was set at 17,000
tons of nitrogen annually. Production began at
FERTISA in 1959, after construction of a plant
whose engineering and installation was supervised
by Montecatini.[8] The total cost of this project
was estimated, at first, to be $12,886,000, includ-
ing share capital totaling $5.5 million, a $4.6 million loan, and credits amounting to $1.3 million.[9]

IFC arranged a loan to FERTISA of $3,886,000
for this project. The loan was to be paid back as
follows: $3,186,000 in semiannual installments
beginning in 1960 and ending in 1969 with interest
of 7 per cent, and $700,000 of interest-free notes
in semiannual installments beginning in 1970 and
ending in 1974.[10] The original agreement called
for IFC to provide $1.4 million of the loan to be
used for additional project capital as well as per-
manent working capital. IFC loaned FERTISA this
amount based on $700,000 of the 7 per cent U.S.
dollar notes maturing in 1969 and $700,000 of the
U.S. dollar income notes maturing between 1970-1974.
These latter notes bore no interest charges but
interest was payable contingent upon earnings being
generated by the project. IFC also received rights
to subscribe to FERTISA shares to be issued in the
future.

Original plans called for a number of foreign
financial institutions to participate in the IFC-
arranged loan. Compagnie Financière de Suez, of
Paris, agreed to purchase $350,000 of IFC's invest-
ment. In addition, Deltec Corporation, a New York
development finance company, participated in the
IFC loan to the planned extent of $1 million.
Handelsfinanz A.G., of Zurich, furnished $1,486,000
of the loan by extending the maturity on an existing
medium-term loan it had made to FERTISA previously.[11]
However, IFC eventually made a net investment, after
participations, of $1,622,000.[12] Apparently either
Compagnie Financière de Suez or Deltec Corporation
reduced its original participation.

After more than a year of operations, FERTISA
began to incur financial problems as a result of

poor profitability. In order to continue production, a reorganization and refinancing of the firm
was decided upon by stockholders and creditors
after meetings in Paris in late 1961 and in Washington early in 1962.

The reorganization was carried out in May,
1962, and consisted of a three-step process: A
significant portion of FERTISA's long-term debt was
readjusted; some interest payments and short-term
debts were funded; and $1,625,000 in new capital
was acquired. The plant's capacity was increased
by 20 per cent after modifications were made and
additional equipment was installed. IFC's contribution to the new capital consisted of an additional
investment of $197,290. This further infusion
brought IFC's total investment in FERTISA to
$4,083,290, or $1,819,290 net of participations.[13]

However, during IFC's tenth fiscal year, it
was reported that FERTISA had defaulted on a principal payment and on some of the interest due.
This was after the company had paid IFC $290,000
toward the principal of the loan. FERTISA had
shown a profit in 1964 but the company reported
lower sales and a loss in 1965.[14] During the IFC
fiscal year 1966-1967, FERTISA met its obligations
on senior debt but remained in default on interest
payments on subordinated debt.[15]

FERTISA, during its 1966 year of operations,
made an attempt to reduce its excessive inventories
and to cut production costs. Company personnel was
reduced by 30 per cent and wages and salaries were
frozen for a two-year period.[16]

In addition to the problems of excessive inventory and declining sales, FERTISA, in 1966, incurred
technical problems in its manufacturing operations.
Malfunctions in the ammonia compressors and the
electrical plant caused interruptions in the manufacturing process.[17] Thus, ammonia production in
1966 declined by 9.3 per cent of that obtained in
1965. The 1966 production of ammonia amounted to
21,747 tons. This represented production of only

80 per cent of estimated 1966 capacity. The production of ammonium sulfate in 1966 was slightly
better than 1965 production and amounted to 14,914
tons. Ammonium nitrate production in 1966 was
37,565 tons. This represented a decline of 10.2
per cent from 1965 output.[18]

Inventories of ammonium sulfate and ammonium
nitrate declined in 1966 from excessive 1965 levels.
The former declined from 2,080 tons in 1965 to 602
tons at the end of 1966. Ammonium nitrate inventories fell from 10,105 tons to 943 tons. Sales of
both these products increased by amounts of 25.9
and 46.2 per cent, respectively. Fertilizer
product-related nitrogen sales increased by 42 per
cent from 1965 to 1966.[19]

However, because of the technical problems in
the manufacturing operations, FERTISA continued to
show a net loss for 1966 of U.S. $115,920 after
allowance for depreciation and payment of debt obligations. In 1965, FERTISA showed a net loss of
$46,383.[20]   Thus, the 1966 net loss deepened much
further from that of 1965.

It appears that FERTISA is making efforts to
cut costs and increase sales. The technical problems which occurred in 1966 are being alleviated.
It appears that some of the cause of these problems
must be attributed to poor management. Steps are
being taken to correct this. The demand for fertilizer and its related products is increasing in
Latin America as agriculture becomes more efficient
and receives more emphasis from Latin American governments and institutions such as the Inter-American
Development Bank and those of the World Bank Group.
The further growth within the Latin American Free
Trade Association will enhance the market for
FERTISA's products. In addition, the reorganization
of the company coupled with IFC's patience and
advice may have enabled FERTISA to survive and to
continue the manufacturing of a product necessary
to the further development of Peru and Latin
America.

However, the wage and salary freeze by FERTISA
may not be maintained because of the relatively
unstable political climate in that part of Latin
America. FERTISA may need more than a financial
reorganization if technical problems continue and
losses increase. Debt obligations will be extremely
difficult to repay and, if FERTISA should have to
cease operations, IFC might have to take a loss in
a Peruvian company for the second time.

PASA, PETROQUIMICA ARGENTINA, S.A.I.C.

One of the largest industrial projects in
Latin America, or in any underdeveloped area, was
planned and built in Argentina. This was a petrochemical plant at San Lorenzo, a small industrial
town located 230 miles up the Parana River from
Buenos Aires. The company, PASA, Petroquimica
Argentina, S.A.I.C., was designed to produce a
broad range of petrochemicals vital to Argentina's
economy including synthetic rubber, benzene, and
chemical intermediates.[21]

Argentina lies between the Andes Mountains and
the Atlantic Ocean and stretches more than 2,000
miles to the southern tip of South America. Border-
ing nations are Bolivia to the northwest, Paraguay
to the northeast, Brazil and Uruguay to the east,
and Chile to the west.

The Argentinian economy is a mixture of pluses
and minuses, mostly the latter. Eighy per cent of
Argentinians, mostly of European descent, live on
the rich fertile pampas which spreads out from
Buenos Aires. Agricultural products, particularly
wheat, corn, and meat, have been Argentina's leading exports. The industrial sector has been underutilized and stagnant because of governmental mis-
management. Serious inflation has been prevalent
in recent years and the devaluation of the Argentine
peso in 1966 was the eighth within two years.
Foreign trade of Argentina is principally with
Great Britain, Italy, and Germany. The transportation system has been allowed to deteriorate badly

under a succession of governments. Argentina could
be classified as stagnant politically and indus-
trially. For a nation whose population is 92 per
cent literate and which has rich natural resources,
this is a sad commentary.[22]

Some sectors within the Argentinian economy
have developed rapidly over the years. One of
these has been the automobile industry. The oil
and natural gas industries have also grown rapidly.
Argentina, before 1961, had been importing rubber
for local manufacture of automobile tires. The
government had completed a 1,200-mile natural gas
pipeline to the San Lorenzo area, 230 miles northwest of Buenos Aires.

A consortium of American companies, including
Continental Oil Company, Cities Service Company,
United States Rubber Company, Fish International
Corporation, and Witco Chemical Company, decided to
construct a petrochemical complex in the San
Lorenzo area to take advantage of the raw material
resources. The complex, PASA, Petroquimica Argentina, S.A., was built to manufacture synthetic
rubber, benzene, and chemical intermediates.

The plant was located near a refinery owned by
Yacimientos Petroliferos Fiscales (YPF). Eventual
annual production estimates called for 45,000 tons
of rubber, 11,300 tons of carbon black, and 6,100
tons of styrene, as well as 8,800 barrels of aviation alkylate, and 850 barrels of benzene daily.[23]
The principal raw materials--natural gas, propane,
and butane--were obtained from YPF.[24]

PASA's sponsors estimated that eventual net
annual savings in foreign exchange to Argentina
would be $29 million as a result of PASA's sales.[25]
The company's principal customer is the automobile
industry whose rubber for tire manufacturing had
been imported. In addition, the benzene and other
petrochemical products opened new local and export
markets.

PASA further benefited the Argentinian economy
by employing over 700 people. Of these, 90 per cent
were Argentinian. The sponsors furnished the initial managerial personnel but agreed to train local
indigents for supervisory positions. In addition,
it was estimated that PASA would spend $14 million
annually for payroll and local raw materials.[26]

The project required $72 million--$63 million
for equipment and installation and $9 million for
prestart-up expense and working capital.[27] The
original project financing consisted of $53,500,000
in debt capital and $18,500,000 in equity capital.
The five sponsors agreed to furnish the equity
capital consisting of $13,500,000 preferred stock
paying a 7.5 per cent dividend and $5 million
common stock representing 85 per cent of the authorized common shares. The sponsors agreed to sell
some of their shares to Argentinian investors after
the plant was in production. A total of $30 mil-
lion was obtained from issuing Class A debentures
to suppliers for machinery and equipment. These
debentures matured in five to seven years and paid
interest of six to eight per cent. Short-term
working capital loans amounting to $5 million were
obtained from local sources.[28]

The remaining $18,500,000 capital was raised
by issuing Class B U.S. dollar subordinated debentures maturing in five to ten years and paying 7.5
per cent interest. Chase International Investment
Corporation, an Edge Act subsidiary of Chase Manhattan Bank, and Lazard Frères & Company, a New
York investment bank, agreed to underwrite the debentures and to purchase some for their own account.
The investing group encouraged seventeen other
American and European financial institutions to
participate in the debentures issue.[29] Among these
were Société Financière de Transports et d'Entre-
prises Industrielles, S.A. (Sofina), Empresas Elec-
tricas Argentinas--a Florida corporation, Keystone
Custodian Funds, Inc., Transoceanic-AOFC, Ltd.,
Philadelphia International Investment Corporation,
Morgan Guaranty International Finance Corporation,
Chemical Overseas Finance Corporation, Bank of

London and South America Ltd., International Holdings Corporation, and the American International Insurance Group.[30]

The Class B debentures were sweetened by a number of special provisions. Warrants were issued which would permit subscription to the stock after the last drawdown on the debentures. Convertibility insurance was provided all U.S. holders by the U.S. Agency for International Development and, when necessary, war-risk and expropriation insurance were furnished. In addition, foreign holders were given the option of drawing principal and interest in either U.S. dollars or Swiss francs if such election was made prior to a certain date.[31] These provisions gave the debentures added marketability.

However, the investment climate in Latin America had been worsening and it appeared that the Class B debenture issue could not be completely sold. At this point, IFC agreed to commit $3,050,000 for the purchase of the remaining unsold Class B debentures. This investment by IFC completed the PASA project financing.

Thus, one of the largest financial investments and one of the largest industrial complexes in any underdeveloped country was completed by nearly complete reliance on private investment. Only a small portion was contributed by a governmental agency and that was the IFC commitment. Financing the project by this method left Argentina the opportunity to acquire much needed funds from foreign and international governmental agencies for other projects.

The PASA project is on stream but has incurred many problems.[32] After conception of the idea, the financing arrangements and engineering plans took four years. Construction began in 1962 and over three years passed before the plant went on stream. Thus, no concrete indication of PASA's profitability is as yet possible. During this period, the project was held up by the Argentinian government, by attacks from competitors, U.S. governmental problems,

difficulties in coordinating U.S. and Argentine
laws, technical and engineering problems, financial
problems raised by banks, sponsors, and vendors,
and the serious political conflict in the Argentinian central government, not to mention the growth
of Castroism in Latin America and its dampening
effect on foreign investment there.

However, the Argentinian government seems
devoted--regardless of internal quarrels--to
private enterprise and to alleviating the nation's
foreign exchange problems. The multinational investment in a project as large as PASA, coupled
with the previously mentioned benefits of the company to Argentina, and the significant markets
which PASA can supply and initiate, points to the
conclusion that the company will be highly successful in the long run and very beneficial to the
whole of Latin America. The problems of PASA have
been overcome and according to an official of Continental Oil Company, one of the sponsors,

> a small group of people have become
> dedicated to the project and are deter-
> mined not to give it up as long as the
> long-run economic outlook for the
> venture remains sound.[33]

COMPAÑIA FUNDIDORA DE FIERRO Y ACERO
DE MONTERREY, S.A. (FUNDIDORA) OF MEXICO

For over fifty years, Mexico has had a relatively stable political system and, during this
period since the nation's last revolution, the
Mexican economy has become one of the strongest in
Latin America. Mexico, or Estado Unidos Mexicanos,
is the largest country in Central America and extends from the southern border of the United States
to British Honduras and Guatemala to the south.
The country is bordered on the west by the Pacific
Ocean and on the east by the Gulf of Mexico.
Mexico's population of over 42,700,000 is divided
thus: 29 per cent is pure-blooded Indian, 61 per
cent mestizo, 9 per cent white, and the remainder

Negroid. This federal republic, comprised of 29 states, has one dominant political party, the Partido Revolucionario Institucional (PRI).

The nation's economy has had a rapid growth rate in recent years but the increase in average annual population of 3.5 per cent has kept the country from furnishing sufficient food needs for its population, although Mexico's economy is predominantly agricultural. Gross national product in 1965 was $19.4 billion, or $478 per capita--one of the highest per capita rates among the developing nations. The average growth rate of Mexico's GNP from 1946 to 1966 was about 5.7 per cent per year. Thus, per capita growth has been over 2 per cent annually. In 1965, agriculture contributed 17.5 per cent to GNP, manufacturing and construction contributed 28.7 per cent, mining and petroleum 5.1 per cent, and all others, mostly services, contributed 48.7 per cent.[34]

Mexico has been one of the World Bank Group's largest customers. Through September, 1966, the World Bank had made sixteen loans to Mexico totaling $625 million. This makes Mexico the World Bank's third largest borrower. Of this amount, 56 per cent was invested in electric power generation and transmission facilities and another $188.5 million went for development of Mexico's transportation system.[35] Mexico has not been eligible for IDA credits because of its relatively high per capita national income.

Mexico has been IFC's second largest customer. During the first decade of operations, IFC made twelve investment commitments in Mexican private enterprises totaling over $21.7 million.[36] About 70 per cent of this total has been acquired by other foreign private financial institutions, either by direct acquisition or by participations, from the United States, Switzerland, Panama, Italy, Kuwait, and Germany.[37] The $21.7 million of IFC investments has assisted investors in financing a total of $104 million of industrial enterprise.

Since IFC's first commitment to a Mexican firm
in 1957, companies in several industries have been
assisted by the institution. Among the products
manufactured by these firms are high speed twist
drills, steel pipes, sodium sulphate, automobile
parts, and steel. IFC's commitment in Tubos de
Acero de Mexico, S.A. (TAMSA) in 1962 represented
the first issue of convertible debentures in Mexico.

The largest total investments made by IFC in a
Mexican firm have been in Compañia Fundidora de
Fierro y Acero de Monterrey, S.A. (Fundidora).
Fundidora is the largest privately owned steel company in Mexico. IFC's three underwriting commitments in 1962, 1964, and 1966 will be discussed in
the remainder of this section.

History of Fundidora

Fundidora was founded in 1900 with a capitalization of $5 million and the company later became
a pioneer in integrated steel production in Latin
America. Thus, the company is among the oldest
firms in which IFC has invested. Operations began
in 1903 with 90,000 tons of production emanating
from a 300-ton blast furnace, a battery of bee-hive
coke ovens, and three small open-hearth furnaces.[38]
The company suffered a shutdown during the Mexican
Revolution of 1913-1915 and by 1929 when the company had regained its pre-Revolution production
level, the world depression began. Finally, the
company began its unending growth in 1932 which has
continued until the present time.

The company began to integrate its operations
vertically by acquiring a large iron ore deposit
at Durango in 1920. Other raw materials producers
have been acquired since then and the company's expansions have included a Monterrey plant for the
manufacture of steel refractories in 1927.[39]
During 1941-1943, Fundidora added a second blast
furnace and enlarged its open-hearth shop. A combination merchant mill was added in 1955.[40]

The Major Expansion: Phase One

In 1957, the company decided on the first of a series of large expansion programs.   Capacity was to be increased from 200,000 to 500,000 tons and production of flat steel was planned.   At that time, the planning called for another expansion in 1962-1965, and one from 1965 to 1970, with a resulting capacity of 1,000,000 tons.   This expansion would necessitate addition of a third blast furnace and four new open-hearth furnaces.

The total cost of the first expansion stage was estimated to be $100 million.   A loan of $42 million had been obtained from the U.S. Export-Import Bank of Washington, D.C.   Nearly all the construction, installation, and engineering work was performed by Fundidora and its subsidiaries.[41] Other capital increases, retained earnings, and borrowings had furnished most of the remaining financial needs.   In addition, the company's directors voted to increase capital stock by an issue of 458,333 shares.   These shares brought in the equivalent of $5.1 million additional funds to Fundidora.

IFC joined with Credito Bursatil, a Mexican investment company, to form an underwriting syndicate for the share issue.   This represented the first underwriting of an equity issue by IFC since its charter was amended to permit such an operation. Shares not subscribed during a rights offering were to be taken up by the syndicate.   Handelsfinanz A.G. of Zurich, Kuhn, Loeb & Company of New York, and Morgan Guaranty International Finance Corporation of New York participated in the underwriting by subscribing to one third of the commitment.[42]   The underwriting was one of the largest in Mexico to that time.

Credito Bursatil, the other member of the syndicate is owned principally by Mexico's largest private bank, Banco Nacional de Mexico.   Shareowners of Credito Bursatil also include Banque de Paris et des Pays-Bas of Paris, Morgan Guaranty International

Finance Corporation, and Banco Hispano-Americano of
Madrid.[43] Credito Bursatil's share of the underwriting was 25 per cent and IFC underwrote the remainder. In addition, IFC agreed to purchase
128,000 Fundidora shares for its own account,
totaling $1.1 million.[44] Thus, IFC's total commit-
ment amounted to $1,126,400 in operational invest-
ments and $2,942,500 underwriting commitment, for a
total of $4,068,900. The shares not subscribed by
Mexican investors during the rights offering were
to be taken up by the syndicate and offered to investors in Latin America, Canada, and Europe.[45]

The Major Expansion: Phase Two

A second phase of Fundidora's long-range goal
of 1,000,000 tons capacity required further financial resources in 1964 since Phase One had been
completed in 1963. This phase, designed to increase
Fundidora's capacity from 500,000 tons to 750,000
tons annually, required an additional increase in
shares outstanding. A new issue of 1,250,000 shares
was voted and priced to yield the equivalent of
$12,500,000. In addition, a loan of $28 million
was obtained from the U.S. Export-Import Bank.
Other funds were generated internally and borrowed
locally.

As in the 1962 financial expansion, IFC joined
with Credito Bursatil, S.A., to underwrite this
issue--the largest in Mexican history. Ten U.S.,
Mexican, and Swiss financial institutions participated in the underwriting syndicate. IFC and
Credito Bursatil shared equally in the new issue
while Kuhn, Loeb & Company, Handelsfinanz A.G., and
Morgan Guaranty International Finance Corporation
participated in IFC's commitment, and seven Mexican
financial institutions participated in Credito Bursatil's commitment. Among these were Banco Nacional
de Mexico, Banco de Comercio, Banco Comercial Mexi-
cano, Banco de Londres y Mexico, Banco Aboumrad,
Banco de Industria y Comercio, and Casasus Trigueros
y Cia.[46]

The new shares were almost completely subscribed during offering with only 8,540 shares
taken up by the syndicate. IFC acquired 34,615
shares at a cost of $346,250 by exercising its
rights. Mexican investors then purchased 25,512
shares of IFC's holdings, reducing IFC's ownership
to 137,103 shares.[47] The total commitment of $6.3
million was the largest made to that date by IFC.

The Major Expansion: Phase Three

In order to meet the goals of 700,000 tons
capacity in 1967, 850,000 tons in 1968, and
1,000,000 tons by 1970, Fundidora required further
external funds in 1966. A new share issue of $7.2
million was made and convertible debentures amounting to $6 million were floated.

For the third time during the decade, Credito
Bursatil joined with IFC to underwrite the new financing. The two institutions equally underwrote
the share issue with Kuhn, Loeb & Company, Morgan
Guaranty International Finance Corporation, and a
member of the Banca Commerciale Italiana Group participating. Kuhn, Loeb participated in the debentures placement with IFC and Credito Bursatil.[48]

The share issue consisted of 750,000 new
shares with rights to buy one new share for each
six held. The convertible debenture issue carries
a 7 per cent coupon, was denominated in U.S.
dollars, matures in 1984, and is convertible into
ordinary shares beginning January 1, 1967.[49]

The new issue was over 99 per cent subscribed.
IFC exercised rights to purchase 16,602 shares at a
cost of $159,443. IFC's original commitment
amounted to $5,883,746.[50]

This financial operation strengthened Fundidora's position in the U.S. and European capital
markets by enhancing the company's credit standing.
The share issue increased Fundidora's stockholders
to well over 2,000 and its stock is now among the
most actively traded on the Mexican Stock Exchanges.[5]

The commitments by IFC raised its total participation in Fundidora since 1962 to $16,402,154. However, because of participations by other financial institutions and sales of investments from its portfolio, IFC held, as of June 30, 1966, only $1,051,219 of the original commitments and this was all in the form of Fundidora shares.[52]

Fundidora and the Mexican Economy

Fundidora's plans for increasing its capacity to 1,000,000 tons are progressing smoothly. The company, the oldest in Latin America, is now the largest steel producer in Mexico. From 1964 to 1965, the company showed a slight decrease in steel production of 3.8 per cent but an increase of 2.23 per cent in finished goods production and a 10.95 per cent increase in net profits on a 1.03 per cent decline in net sales.[53] The reduction in sales resulted from requirements of 16,000 tons of finished materials for the expansion program.

By summer, 1967, Fundidora had a number of the new expansion projects on stream. Among these are No. 3 and No. 4 open-hearth furnaces, a No. 3 blast furnace, a 26-inch billet mill, a 54-inch tandem cold mill, a welded structural shapes department, and a rail mill. Since 1945 Fundidora has been unable to supply Mexican needs for new rails; thus, the National Railroad of Mexico has had to import large deliveries of rails.[54] In addition to these additions and the further objective of 1,000,000 tons capacity by 1970, the company is discussing production of 2,000,000 tons by 1975.[55]

The Fundidora plant is among the most modern in the developing countries. The Ross Report recommends the purchase of Fundidora shares as a means of participating in a growth situation for many years to come.[56] This report shows that sales increased to 826 million pesos (approximately $66.1 million) in 1966, a 17.2 per cent increase over 1965, and furthermore, 1967 sales should increase by another 35 per cent.[57]

Fundidora's growth and expansion program has benefited Mexico in several ways. From 1964 to 1965, Mexican steel production increased by 5.5 per cent but imports of steel increased by 36.7 per cent. Mexican exports increased during this period by 27.1 per cent but are only about one half Mexican steel imports and the latter were 14.1 per cent of domestic consumption in 1965.[58] Therefore, the increase by Fundidora in finished steel products manufactured will enable Mexico to increase exports of these products. The large expansion in steel production will reduce the need for Mexico to use foreign exchange for steel imports. The company has integrated production to the point where raw materials imports are not needed. The company and its subsidiaries employ 17,000 persons and these companies have raised productivity of their workers by building company homes, implementing health programs, and maintaining good labor relations.

The financing of this expansion has resulted in improving and expanding the market for Fundidora's shares. The market for these shares in Mexico has been enhanced by increased shareownership by Mexicans. Shareowners of Fundidora stock have more than tripled since 1962, from 700 to over 2,000 at present. The $4 million share issue in 1962 was only 60 per cent subscribed during the offering period but the 1964 offering of over $12 million was completely subscribed. Thus, in two years the Mexican market had become able to absorb such an issue.[59] The stock is now one of the most actively traded on the Mexico City Exchange. The convertible debenture issue will enable Fundidora to enter foreign capital markets for funds. Furthermore, several foreign private financial institutions have been encouraged by IFC to participate in Fundidora's financial needs. IFC, thus, has been able to facilitate an expansion which has greatly benefited a growing economy and has been able to fulfill most of its objectives in assisting Fundidora.

ACOS VILLARES, S.A., OF BRAZIL

The International Finance Corporation's commitment in Acos Villares, S.A., a specialty steel
producer, is one of eight IFC investments in Brazilian companies and these commitments date back
to the first year of IFC operations when the institution assisted Siemens do Brasil Companhia de Elec-
tricidade, a heavy electrical equipment manufacturer. Since then, IFC's eight commitments in
Brazil during the period 1956-1966 have totaled
$22,483,949. No other country has received a
higher amount of investment from IFC. This total
represents about 22 per cent of funds committed by
IFC in Latin America and 13 per cent of IFC's total
committed funds.

Brazil's area of 3,286,170 square miles covers
almost half the Latin American continent and the
country borders on ten other South American nations.
Its population of 84.5 million was growing at an
annual rate of 2.4 per cent in 1966.

The economy of Brazil is divided as follows:
28 per cent agricultural and fishing, 28 per cent
industrial and mining, and 44 per cent government
and services. Brazilian gross national product has
increased at the rapid average annual rate of 5.7
per cent from 1947 to 1966 and per capita national
income was estimated to be $200-250 in the latter
year.[60]

The World Bank Group has been very active in
Brazil with twenty loans approved for the nation by
June 30, 1967, totaling $496 million. Thus, Brazil
is the Bank's fourth largest borrower in the world.[61]
The bulk of these loans, seventeen for $446 million,
has been for electric power development.[62]

Brazil's industrial output increased 10 per
cent annually from 1947 to 1962. A diversification
program has beem implemented in recent years. However, political instability resulting in extremely
high rates of inflation has plagued Brazil during

the 1960's.   The nation has incurred general price increases of 50-100 per cent in a single year.

Rapid industrialization and its diversification have contributed to the inflation although long-term industrial growth will enable Brazil to allocate investment so that the inflationary pressures will be alleviated.   In turn, the steady drain on the nation's scarce foreign exchange reserves caused by the rising consumer demand will be reduced.

Among the fastest growing industries in Brazil is the automobile industry.   Rapid growth in this and other industries has increased the domestic needs for special steel and related products.   In late 1965, IFC announced a $5,051,068 investment in Acos Villares, S.A., a special steels producer located in São Paulo.   IFC had made six previous investments in Brazilian companies but none of these had been made since 1959.   Business investment opportunities between 1959 and 1965 had been considered too risky by the World Bank Group.

Acos Villares employs over 2,000 workers and produces several types of special and alloy steels and iron and steel products.   Among the latter are castings and rolling mill rolls.   The company was founded by the Villares family, well known in Brazil, and was privately held until 1959.   Since a public share offering then, more than 1,200 shareholders have participated in ownership of the company and Acos Villares shares are now actively traded on both the Rio de Janeiro and São Paulo Stock Exchanges.[63]

The announced investment by IFC is to assist in a $7.3 million expansion program during which Acos Villares will increase its annual ingot steel capacity from 54,000 tons to 63,000 tons and its production of finished steel products including rolling mill rolls and high quality tools and stainless steels.[64]

IFC's investment consisted of a loan of $4 million maturing in 14 years and subscriptions to preferred and common stock of Acos Villares totaling $1,051,068.[65] The remaining portion of the project's cost is being financed by assistance from the National Development Bank of Brazil and by internal generation of funds. In addition, American, Austrian, and French steel companies agreed to furnish technical assistance.[66]

At the present time, an evaluation of the investment would be premature. The expansion project is presently being implemented and construction apparently will not be completed until 1968.[67] However, the commitment supplied the major portion of the financing of a project which will help satisfy the demand of the Brazilian automotive industry for specialty steel and that of Brazil's steel industry for rolling mill rolls. The financing by IFC also marked a renewal in assistance to private enterprise in Brazil. Thus, the World Bank Group apparently decided that the investment climate in Brazil showed marked improvement by 1965.

PAPEL E CELULOSE CATARINENSE, S.A.

Shortly after the investment in Acos Villares, IFC announced approval of an investment proposal submitted by Papel e Celulose Catarinense, S.A., for a new $26 million kraft pulp and paper mill to be located near Lajes in the state of Santa Catarina, south of Saõ Paulo.[68]

The new mill is being constructed with annual capacity of 47,000 tons of bleached and unbleached kraft paper and 10,000 tons of kraft pulp. The waste from local logging and saw mill operations will furnish the mill's raw materials until pine plantations can be established by the company.[69] Self-sufficiency in raw materials is intended within 20 years.

The Klabin group in Brazil, now engaged in production of newsprint, container board, and kraft

paper, is sponsoring the project. This group is
one of Brazil's leading industrial interests and
has produced paper in Brazil since 1906. The group
also has interests in ceramic tile manufacturing,
chemicals, electrical appliances, mining, ranching,
and coffee growing.[70]

The project's cost of $26 million is being fi-
nanced with a $13.2 million share issue and loans
totaling $12.8 million. The shares were subscribed
as follows: $8.8 million by the sponsors and
Montei Aranha, another Brazilian industrial group;
$2.9 million by IFC; and $1.5 million by Adela Investment Company S.A. of Luxembourg. In addition,
the shareholders agreed to cover production cost
overruns up to $1 million in proportion to their
holdings. IFC's commitment on overruns would
amount to approximately $307,881.

The debt financing of the project is as follows:
a long-term loan from the National Development Bank
of Brazil (BNDE) of $5.5 million; a long-term loan
of $3.3 million from the Inter-American Development
Bank; and a ten-year $2.5 million loan from IFC.
In addition, BNDE is providing a standby loan of
$850,000 and the Klabin group and IFC each have
committed $425,000 standby loans. The Bank of
America, New York, a subsidiary of Bank of America,
N.T. & S.A., is participating in the IFC commitment.[71]

These loan agreements all mature in ten years
and have three-year grace periods. The IFC loan
carries an interest rate of 8 per cent and the loan
from the Inter-American Development Bank (IDB) has
an interest rate of 6 per cent. Both are denominated in dollars and the IDB loan has been guaranteed by BNDE. The BNDE loan carries an interest
charge of 12 per cent, contains a maintenance-of-
value clause to protect the lender against inflation, and is denominated in cruzeiros.[72]

The $26 million mill, financed by international
interests, consists of components manufactured in
several countries. The pulp mill was ordered in
Finland; the steam and power plant is being manu-

factured by a Swedish company; the paper mill is
Italian. The pulp mill will be able to pulp soft-
wood and hardwood in any proportion and will be
self-sufficient in steam and power generation. The
plant will include a complete chemical recovery
system and a chlorine dioxide generating plant.[73]

Production will not begin before 1969. Ground
was broken in Fall, 1966, and building construction
began in May, 1967. The pulp mill assembly was
begun in Fall, 1967, and paper mill construction
was started in early 1968. The former will go
on stream in November, 1968, and plans are for the
latter to go on stream in early 1969.[74] Thus, no
specific assessment of the mill's operations can be
made at the time of this writing.

Some predictions can be made, however, of the
benefits which will accrue to the Brazilian economy
from this project. The entire integrated operation
will employ over 1,600 workers and will help raise
local per capita income in Santa Catarina where it
is estimated to be half the national average. The
existing domestic demand for paper will be partially
satisfied by the mill and packaging materials, such
as multiwall sacks and wrapping paper, will assist
the packaged goods industries. In addition, Brazil
will require less imported pulp and, thus, a foreign
exchange savings will result.[75]

IFC has been able to fulfill some of its objectives by this investment commitment. Foreign
private financial institutions have been encouraged
to participate and its portfolio has been diversified by industry. In addition, IFC has helped to
promote a project which was conceived in 1957 and
for which firm orders for machinery had been placed
with Scandinavian firms. Sponsors and the Inter-
American Development Bank had assisted the financing
of these purchases. However, IFC had turned down a
proposal for investment funds in 1962 because of
the bleak economic situation at that time in Brazil.
IFC reappraised the project, proposed a revamped
financial plan, and approved the proposal when the
sponsors applied again for IFC assistance in 1965.[76]

Finally, this commitment represented one of the largest single investments in a project by IFC during its first decade of operations.

IFC COMMITMENTS TO PRIVATE DEVELOPMENT FINANCE COMPANIES IN LATIN AMERICA

The first investments by IFC in private development financial institutions were made in two Colombian companies in 1961. Since then, IFC has invested in a third Colombian company and in a Venezuelan financing company. By the end of its tenth fiscal year, IFC had made these four commitments in Latin American private development finance companies totaling $6,103,316.[77]

Corporación Financiera Colombiana de Desarrollo Industrial (Bogota) and Corporación Financiera Nacional (Medellin)

The first of these, as mentioned, were made in 1961 to the Corporación Financiera Colombiana de Desarrollo Industrial, of Bogota, and the Corporación Financiera Nacional, of Medellin. These institutions were established in 1958 and 1959, respectively, to provide medium- and long-term industrial development capital and to assist the development of the Colombian capital market. Until the IFC investment, the two institutions had engaged in only medium-term operations. The companies' stock is owned by Colombian banks, insurance companies, industrial firms, and private individuals.[78]

The IFC investments to both companies were made in the form of notes bearing no fixed interest, maturing between 1971 and 1973, and fully convertible into common stock. The notes were unsecured and interest equal to dividends on common stock was payable.[79] IFC subsequently converted the equivalent of $3,999,452 of these notes into common shares of the two companies. This represented the first holding of shares by IFC since its charter was amended in 1961 permitting such operations.[80]

C.A. Venezolana de Desarrollo (Sociedad Financiera)

In October, 1963, IFC participated with over
eighty Venezuelan and foreign investors to form
C.A. Venezolana de Desarrollo (CAVENDES), a private
development finance company established for the
purpose of financing industrialization in Venezuela
outside the areas of mining and petroleum. The
principal sponsor was Corporación Venezolana de
Fomento (CVF), a government-owned development bank.
Among the other subscribers to the company's shares
were Inversiónes Shell de Venezuela; Manufacturers
Hanover Trust Company; First National City Bank;
Chemical International Finance, Ltd.; Northwest
International Bank; commercial banks and oil companies of the United Kingdom, Germany, Italy, Netherlands, and the United States; and leading Venezuelan banks and businessmen.[81]

The new institution was formed with share capital of $8.1 million of which CVF and IFC both sub-
scribed $1.33 million.[82] IFC's interest amounted
to 15 per cent of the ownership, or 60,000 shares.[83]

This new institution is assisting industrialization of Venezuela in many ways. The diversification of its commitments reduces the reliance of
the nation on the petroleum sector. The company is
pioneering in underwriting new issues in Venezuela.[84]
The company made loans totaling $29.9 million and
participated in six underwriting operations between
January, 1964, and the end of September, 1967.
These investments assisted companies in such industries as foodstuffs, paper, textiles, and light
metallurgy.[85]

Corporación Financiera de Caldas of Colombia

The Corporación Financiera de Caldas, located
in Manizales in the Department of Caldas, was
formed in 1961 to assist in the diversification of
a local economy which was producing one third of
Colombia's coffee output. Its shares are held by

over 200 investors including the National Federation of Coffee Growers, the Federation's regional committees in the Departments of Caldas and Tolima, the Banco Cafetero, and the Banco del Comercio, one of Colombia's leading banks.[86]

IFC's investment in this financiera took the form of a subscription to 70,000 shares valued at $701,403. Existing shareholders had just previously subscribed to approximately $670,000 of shares and the IFC investment was followed by share commitments by Wells Fargo Bank International Corporation and The Company for Investing Abroad, a subsidiary of the Fidelity Philadelphia Trust Company.[87] These investments increased the company's share capital to $4.2 million.

The area had incurred rapid industrial growth during the period preceding establishment of the Caldas Financiera. This industrialization has continued since its formation and the financiera's operations in the small business area as well as its sponsoring of a new chemical plant and two mining companies have all contributed to this industrialization and diversification of Colombia's economy. As of December 31, 1963, Caldas Financiera's investment portfolio of loans and equities amounted to nearly $6.8 million.[88] The company's promotional efforts are enhanced by the growth prospects in the Caldas region, principally in the mining and forestry products industries.

Summary

A number of IFC's objectives have been fulfilled by these investments in private development finance companies. These companies have been able to assist smaller companies with smaller investments than IFC normally would consider. A number of new industrial firms have been promoted by the activities of these institutions, and diversification of the Colombian and Venezuelan economies has resulted. Foreign private financial institutions have been encouraged to participate in these projects and local capital markets have been improved.

CHAPTER **6** THE INTERNATIONAL
FINANCE CORPORATION
IN ASIA AND THE
MIDDLE EAST

INTRODUCTION

The IFC has committed more funds in Asia and
the Middle East than in any other geographical
region except Latin America. After ten years of
operations, IFC had made twenty-two commitments to
this area totaling $31,403,740.[1] The IFC activity
in this area represents only a little over one sixth
of IFC's total commitments and about 18 per cent of
total funds committed by the institution. Table 7
shows a breakdown of IFC activities in this area by
country.

Although IFC has committed more than three
times as many funds to the Latin American countries
as to Asian countries, the institution has begun in
recent years to show an increasing interest in
Asian economic development. The first activities
of IFC were in the Western Hemisphere and, naturally,
some expertise arose from investing in South America.
However, a goal of IFC has always been to develop a
diversified portfolio not only by industries but
also by geographic regions and countries. Therefore,
more emphasis has been placed on investments in Asia
in recent years. In fact, ten of the twenty-two
commitments have been made during the last three
fiscal years for a total of $16,009,162, slightly
over half the total funds invested by IFC in Asia
and the Middle East since 1956.

Table 7

IFC Investment, Standby and
Underwriting Commitments, 1956-1966,
Asia and the Middle East

Country	Initial Commitment	No. of Commitments	Funds Committed
India	1959	9	$ 10,775,802
Iran	1959	1	300,000
Malaysia	1963	2	2,867,298
Pakistan	1958	7	12,608,469
Philippines	1962	1	4,359,063
Thailand	1959	2	493,108
		22	$ 31,403,740

Source: IFC, Annual Report 1965-1966 (Washington,
         D.C.: International Finance Corporation,
         1966), p. 4.

The IFC has made investments to both industrial
firms and to development banks in this area. Table
8 shows that eighteen investments have been made in
sixteen industrial companies and four have been
made in development finance companies. Second commitments have been made in Ismail Cement Industries,
Ltd., of Pakistan and in Precision Bearings India,
Ltd., of India.

The purpose of the remainder of this chapter
is to examine in greater detail a number of individual cases in which IFC has participated in the
Asian area. Three industrial investments are analyzed. These are Mahindra Ugine Steel Company, Ltd.
of India and Ismail Cement Industries, Ltd. and
Packages, Ltd. of Pakistan. These companies were
selected for a number of reasons. Ismail and
Mahindra-Ugine were companies established at the
time of the IFC investments. Packages, Ltd. was an
established company but one needing expansion capital. Local private development finance companies
participated in each investment. Packages, with

Swedish influence, and Mahindra-Ugine, with French interests, were formed as joint international business ventures.   Finally, IFC's investment in Ismail Cement is the largest commitment by that institution in Asia.   The four commitments made to private development finance companies in India, Malaysia, Pakistan, and Thailand are discussed in some detail. Some attempt is made to evaluate each of the investments in terms of current operations of the companies and the contribution of each company to its national economy.

ISMAIL CEMENT INDUSTRIES, LTD.[2]

Pakistan is a nation covering 365,528 square miles with a population of over 103 million.   Thus, it is one of the largest and most populous of the developing economies.   The country is divided by India into two areas about 1,000 miles apart.   The country has a federal government and has had serious troubles with India over disputed possession of the Kashmir region.   War has occasionally erupted over this matter.

Pakistan initiated its third five-year economic plan in 1965.   Industrialization has been ambitiously supported but the country remains predominantly an agricultural economy.   Pakistan is a leading jute and cotton exporter and wood is also an important export product.

Pakistan, being one of the developing countries of the world, has had a dynamic construction industry in the last few years because of the emphasis on industrialization.   Demand for cement has exceeded the supply.   Thus, some construction shortages have occurred and cement has had to be imported by Pakistan, thus necessitating use of scarce foreign exchange.

Ismail Cement Industries, Ltd., was organized in 1960 by Naseer A. Shaikh, present chairman of the company's board, and other Pakistani industrialists.   A large increase in cement demand had been

Table 8

IFC Commitments in Asia by Company

Company	Country	Operation-al Invest-ment	Standby and Under-writing
Republic Forge Co., Ltd.	India	$ 1,500,000	$ ---
Kirloskar Oil Engine Ltd.	"	850,000	---
Assam Sillimanite, Ltd.	"	1,365,000	---
K.S.B. Pumps, Ltd.	"	210,000	---
Precision Bearings, Ltd.	"	1,030,197	---
Fort Gloster Industries, Ltd.	"	1,211,047	---
Mahindra Ugine Steel Co., Ltd. (MUSCO)	"	3,296,840	---
Lakshmi Machine Works, Ltd.	"	1,312,718	---
Sherkate Sahami Kahkashan	Iran	300,000	---
Malaysian Industrial Development Finance, Ltd.	Malaysia	817,917	490,000
Tasek Cement, Ltd.	"	1,559,381	---

Steel Corporation of Pakistan, Ltd.	Pakistan	630,000	---
Adamjee Industries, Ltd.	"	750,000	---
Ismail Cement Industries, Ltd.	"	5,677,417	---
Pakistan Industrial Credit and Investment Corp., Ltd.	"	449,400	---
Crescent Jute Products, Ltd.	"	1,950,000	---
Packages, Ltd.	"	3,151,662	---
Private Development Corp. of the Philippines	Philippines	---	4,359,063
Concrete Products and Aggregate Co., Ltd.	Thailand	300,000	---
Industrial Finance Corp. of Thailand	"	193,108	---
Totals		$26,554,677	$4,849,063

Source: IFC, Annual Report 1965-1966 (Washington, D.C.: International Finance Corporation, 1966), Appendix C, pp. 35, 36, and 38.

107

expected because of major construction projects
planned for the Indus River Basin development program. After the Indian-Pakistani partition, only
four cement plants remained in West Pakistan. All
were Indian-owned with foreign exchange restrictions in effect between the two countries, and none
of these plants could be expanded to meet the increased demand.

Ismail carried out construction of a Portland
cement plant near Ismailwal (formerly Gharibwal),
West Pakistan. The plant consisted of two kilns
with annual capacity of 400,000 tons of cement.
Railway and highway connections to the factory site
were built by the Pakistani government. Total cost
of the plant was estimated to be $12,275,000.

The funds needed to finance this project were
obtained from a number of sources. Mr. Shaikh and
other sponsors contributed some capital and an over-
subscribed public share issue totaling 11 million
rupees ($2,328,042) was made in Pakistan. A total
of $5,275,000 was raised in this manner. Applica-
tion was made to IFC for an investment commitment.
IFC and the Pakistan Industrial Credit and Investment Corporation Ltd. (PICIC) entered into a joint
investment agreement to furnish the foreign exchange requirements of $7 million. The IFC commit-
ment totaled $4 million and PICIC invested $3
million.

IFC invested the following package: $2,750,000
in dollar debentures bearing 7.5 per cent interest
and maturing between 1966-1973, and $1,250,000 in
convertible dollar income notes which were entitled
to income, in rupees, equal to dividends on an
equivalent amount of stock.[3]

PICIC loaned Ismail $3 million, taking deben-
tures bearing 7.5 per cent interest, maturing between 1966-1973, and carrying a maintenance-of-
value clause in the indenture. The proceeds for
this loan by PICIC came from a loan by the World
Bank to the development finance company.

PICIC also participated in the equity of Ismail
by taking shares amounting to 2,850,000 rupees and
agreed to a standby commitment in the public issue
of Ismail shares amounting to 11 million rupees.

The construction industry in Pakistan continued to require increasing amounts of cement.
Ismail directors decided in 1965 to expand the
plant's capacity from 416,000 tons annually to
642,000 tons. To facilitate this expansion and
other company needs, investment capital amounting
to $5,800,000 was required. The original plant was
begun in 1962 with production starting in mid-1964,
and the expansion called for addition of a third
kiln and auxiliary equipment. Part of the financial needs was to be financed from internal operations.

IFC and PICIC entered into a joint investment
agreement for the second time with Ismail. IFC
agreed to invest $1,677,000 by subscribing to shares
in the amount of $417,000 and the making of a loan
denominated in dollars and sterling of $1,134,000
and £45,000. PICIC's commitment was for a subscription to shares in the same amount as IFC's
subscription, with a loan of slightly more than
$1 million.

IFC's objective of encouraging other financial
institutions to participate in its investments was
demonstrated in the Ismail case. The Bank of America N.T. and S.A. of San Francisco participated in
the first IFC commitment in the amount of $172,000,
and Continental International Finance Corporation,
an affiliate of Continental Illinois National Bank
and Trust Company of Chicago, also purchased part
of the 1961 IFC loan. The National and Grindlays
Bank Limited of London participated in the 1965 IFC
investment in Ismail.

The two IFC commitments totaled $5,677,407 and
this amount was the largest investment by IFC in
Asia as of June, 1966. Of this amount, slightly
over $400,000 represents equity IFC holds in Ismail
and almost $400,000 of IFC's loans has been sold to

other financial institutions. During fiscal year 1966, Ismail paid back an equivalent of approximately $360,000 on the loan and had plans to remit such an amount in October, 1966, and again in April, 1967.[4]

A perusal of Ismail's annual report for the year ending June 30, 1966, the second year of operations, reveals that the company made a <u>gross profit</u> of 8,795,964 rupees (approximately $1,850,000 However, a fair evaluation is difficult because of some accounting practices used by the company such as capitalizing some interest expense and not including depreciation in the profit and loss statement. The gross profit also includes income of "casual nature" amounting to 1,341,173 rupees.

Ismail's operations could have been better during the second year of operations but during the early part of the year, the India-Pakistani war was being waged and some operations were hindered by the shortage of fuel.

However, the company's operations and sales should benefit from the rise in construction activity in West Pakistan. Exports of cement to East Pakistan and foreign countries are being allowed. The Pakistani government has estimated that production of cement in Pakistan will have to rise from a 1964-1965 output of 2,200,000 tons to a 1969-1970 output of 5 million tons if demand is to be satisfied. Therefore, Ismail appears to be situated in a growth industry and, if managed well, the company's operations should justify the IFC commitment.

MAHINDRA UGINE STEEL COMPANY LIMITED (MUSCO)

India has the largest population of the free-world nations with 486,700,000 crowded into an area of 1,229,215 square miles. This figure includes the area of the disputed state of Kashmir. India is a member of the British Commonwealth and has a socialist-oriented parliamentary government with states being administered by presidentially appointed governors.

The economy suffers from overpopulation and is basically agricultural. Famine is still quite common because of drought and bureaucratic inefficiencies. Without food shipments from the industrialized nations, India probably could not survive. The nation has large amounts of underutilized natural resources and has been implementing economic planning for a number of years. However, with population estimated to be 1 billion by the year 2000, food problems will become even more severe.

The Indian economy is undergoing development pains and its foreign exchange reserves are quite limited. The rapid increase in industrial production programmed for the current five-year plan will increase the steel requirements of the Indian economy. Between 1959 and 1962, the output of common steel doubled.[5]

The Indian government gave high priority to developing the means of production of alloy steels to complement the common steel output. Imports of alloy steel had increased and foreign exchange reserves were needed for these imports even though controls were placed on such imports. Thus, Indian and French industrial interests were encouraged to plan the construction and operation of an alloy steel plant at Khopoli, located sixty-five miles from Bombay in the State of Maharashtra. The plant was planned to serve the Bombay industrial area which, with the Calcutta area, is one of the leading industrial centers in India.

The site was selected because of its soil conditions, availability of power and water, and easy access to transportation facilities, as well as its proximity to industrial centers. Melting scrap, an important raw material, would be available because of the rapid growth of steel consuming factories in western India.[6]

A new company, the Mahindra Ugine Steel Company Limited (MUSCO), was formed for the purpose of building and operating the plant. Its Indian sponsor is Mahindra and Mahindra Limited, of Bombay, a

manufacturer of jeeps, trailers, agricultural tractors and implements, Diesel engines, and textile
machinery, as well as importer and distributor of
steel in India. The French sponsor is Société
d'Electro-Chimie, d'Electro-Metallurgie et des
Acieries Electriques d'Ugine (Ugine), a principal
alloy steel maker. A subsidiary company, Société
Inde-Ugine, has been formed to hold a participation
in MUSCO by Ugine together with Compagnie Financière de Suez in Paris and the Comptoir National
d'Escompte de Paris.

The new plant was planned to have an annual
capacity of 18,000 tons of finished alloy steel
products with future expansion possible; however,
the finished plant will produce 24,000 tons and
can be expanded to 36,000 tons capacity. The
plant's ingot capacity will be 50,000 tons if
alloy steel is not produced. MUSCO began production in 1966.

Financial requirements of the project amounted
to 65 million rupees (approximately $13,650,000),
half of which was to be financed by long-term loans.
The remainder came from an initial stock issue of
common and preference shares totaling 30 million
rupees, and 2,500,000 rupees in suppliers' credits.
The financial breakdown is given in Table 9. IFC
also made a contingent equity investment of $300,000
if an additional share issue might be needed because
of underestimated costs. Thus IFC's contribution
amounted to slightly less than one fourth of the
total project cost and consisted of the loan of
$2.31 million and a subscription to shares whose
equivalent value was $845,000. This, with the
standby, totaled $3,450,001 which IFC invested in
the project.

As is shown in Table 9, two sources of MUSCO
financing were Indian development institutions.
The Industrial Finance Corporation of India (IFCI),
a government-sponsored institution, supplied loan
capital amounting to 15 million rupees. Also, the
Industrial Credit and Investment Corporation of
India (ICICI), a privately owned development finance

Table 9

Financial Program for MUSCO
(thousands of rupees)

Share Capital	
Common Shares	
IFC	4,000
Indian sponsors	6,150
Foreign sponsors	4,150
Indian public and	
Underwriters	10,700
Preference Shares	
Indian institutions	5,000
Total Equity	30,000
Long-Term Loans	
ICICI	6,500
IFCI	15,000
IFC	11,000
Suppliers' Credits	2,500
Total Loans	35,000
Total	65,000

Source: IFC, Annual Report 1963-1964 (Washington,
         D.C.: International Finance Corporation,
         1964), p. 23.

company, loaned MUSCO 6.5 million rupees. The
latter loan came from foreign exchange resources
loaned to ICICI by the World Bank.

The conditions of the IFC investment are
typical of the institution's financial terms.[7]
The rate of interest on the loan is 7 per cent.
The loan is repayable in twenty semiannual equal
installments. MUSCO has to pay IFC a semiannual
commitment charge of 1 per cent per annum on the
principal amount of the loan undisbursed to MUSCO.
The financial assistance to MUSCO by IFC relates to
the construction, equipment, and operation of, and
provision of working capital for, a plant with an

annual production of 24,000 tons of finished tool,
alloy, and special steels and related products.

Under the investment agreement, IFC subscribed
to 400,000 shares of MUSCO common stock. The shares
were subscribed to in the ratio of 20,000 shares
for each $115,500 of disbursement under the loan
requested by MUSCO.

IFC has encouraged participation by other financial institutions in this investment. The Continental International Finance Corporation, a
subsidiary of the Continental Illinois National
Bank and Trust Company of Chicago, participated in
the investment to the extent of $150,000.

An evaluation of the progress of MUSCO is
difficult to make. Construction in earnest began
in 1965.[8] During the first year, a rolling mill,
a forge, and a shipping building had been built.
Buildings for melting and heat treatment as well
as for finishing were nearing completion in 1966.
Other ancillary buildings have been completed. Test
runs for rolling of alloy steel were begun in late
1966. Orders by indigenous importers have been
placed with MUSCO and the Indian government will
probably limit imports of the type steels to be
produced by MUSCO.

At present, the plant consists of a number of
departments. They are a steel melting shop, a
forge, a rolling mill, a heat treatment and finishing shop, and a storage and shipping department.
Modern machinery has been installed at MUSCO, including a 20-ton electric arc furnace, a 5-ton
electric arc and slag furnace, a 1,200-ton forging
press with two mobile manipulators, pneumatic
hammers, a walking furnace for reheating, a rolling
mill, and annealing and quenching furnaces. Ultra-
sonic inspection equipment has been installed and
the plant utilizes the Ugine-Perrin method for
accelerating the processes of de-oxidization and
desulphurization in the manufacturing of special
steels. MUSCO is also completing research facilities in its own laboratory.[9]

Although the original total cost estimate of the project has been exceeded by several million rupees, a large foreign exchange savings will result because of the lessened requirements for special alloy steel imports. At full capacity, these savings have been estimated at 60 million rupees annually.[10]

PACKAGES, LTD.

One of the leading economic indicators in any nation is paperboard production because goods have to be packaged. Pakistan has had a growing demand for packaging materials including paperboard. Before 1957, most of the packaging materials used in Pakistan were imported. This practice consumed scarce foreign exchange reserves. By 1955, Pakistan had three paper and board mills in production and the need to convert some of this production to the manufacture of packaging materials was recognized by government officials. A new enterprise, Packages, Ltd., was formed for the purpose of filling this gap. Two leading European companies combined efforts with a leading Pakistani business group to form Packages, Ltd. Akerlund & Rausing, a leading packaging materials manufacturer located in Sweden, and G.-Man, the leading ink manufacturer in northern Europe, combined with the House of Wazir Ali, a family firm founded in Pakistan in 1858. The Wazir Ali group has interests in manufacturing, processing, and service industries including automobile, motor scooter and tractor assembly, cotton textiles, soap manufacturing, and insurance.

Construction of the plant began in 1956 and manufacturing operations began in April, 1957. Technical advice and training of Pakistani personnel was undertaken by Akerlund & Rausing.

The company first supplied containers and packages principally to the cigarette and soap industries. Since 1957, it has diversified its manufacturing until it now provides packaging materials for 40 different industries.

In 1965, company officials decided on an expansion program to be carried out at the Packages plant in Lahore, West Pakistan. The expansion, estimated at 60,380,000 rupees (equivalent to $12,680,000), included construction of an integrated pulp and paperboard mill adjacent to the facilities for converting paperboard into packages and containers. This mill was planned to have an annual capacity of 15,000 tons and the capacity of the converting operations was increased from 12,000 tons to 18,000 tons. Locally obtained raw materials--wheat straw and cotton linters--are used to make the paperboard.

This expansion project was brought to the attention of IFC by the Pakistan Industrial Credit and Investment Corporation (PICIC). IFC decided to enter a joint agreement with PICIC to contribute to the project. The two institutions had jointly assisted the Ismail Cement Industries project. PICIC's loan to Packages was to assist the company in purchasing machinery and equipment abroad. Part of the PICIC loan was from a World Bank line of credit and part was from a Japanese government yen loan, as can be seen in Table 10.[11] The items marked by asterisks in Table 10 were not budgeted for in the original 1965 request for funds but apparently were results of underestimating expenditures for the expansion. The public share issue of 10 million rupees was a result of the conversion of the company into a publicly owned enterprise and represented a secondary offering of shares held by the sponsors. The IFC investment was equivalent to $2,310,000 on the loan and $840,001 on the subscription to shares. The Stockholms Enskilda Bank of Stockholm and The Chartered Bank of London participated in the investment.[12]

Packages, Ltd. has had a fairly profitable background and appears to have a good future ahead. The nine-year summary of operations 1958-1966 shows that sales have increased in each successive year and quadrupled during the entire period. Profits after taxes have more than tripled during the period and only in 1962 and 1963 were profits lower

Table 10

Financial Program for Packages Expansion
Sources of Finance--Paperboard Project
(thousands of rupees)

Long-term Debt:	
PICIC Loan in Yen	7,149
PICIC Loan in Foreign Currency	5,050
*PICIC Loan (now requested)	3,030
IFC Loan	11,111
Rupee Debentures to be Placed	
in Pakistan	2,000
*Rupee Debentures for Customs Duty	3,400
Equity Ordinary Shares:	
Wazir Ali	4,500
Akerlund & Rausing	4,000
IFC	4,000
Public issue	10,000
*Payment by Abbasi Textile Mills	750
Cash Generation up to June, 1967	11,881
*Bank Overdraft	12,479
*Rupee Borrowing for New Overrun	2,200
Total Expenditure Budgeted	81,550

Source: From correspondence sent June 10, 1967, by
          Syed Irshad Hussain, Director and General
          Manager, Packages, Ltd.

than the preceding year. Packages' profit margin
after taxes has a range from a low of 4.2 per cent
to a high of 12.1 per cent and the nine-year average
is 8.74 per cent. Dividends totaling 2,231,000
rupees were paid during 1960-1964 and fixed assets,
depreciated, have increased more than tenfold over
the period.[13] The 1966 profit figure pertains to
the Packaging Division and includes no operations
of the Paper-Board Mill expansion project. One new
paper machine started operations in June, 1967, and
two more were planned to start operating in August,
1967, about a year ahead of normal construction
schedules for projects of this type.[14]

Thus, it appears that Packages, Ltd. will continue to be successful in the future. The company's operations are quite diversified and have now been significantly expanded. Pakistani management and Swedish technical advice have combined to produce good financial results.

The IFC investment appears to be sound and the institution has again been successful in fulfilling its objectives of encouraging local and foreign financial institutions to participate in the economic development process. IFC has joined again with a local private development finance company to assist in filling a need in a developing nation.

IFC COMMITMENTS TO ASIAN DEVELOPMENT FINANCE COMPANIES

IFC took the lead for the World Bank Group in 1962 in assisting industrial development finance companies. During the period ending June 30, 1966, IFC had assisted four such companies in the Asia-Middle East area. They were the Malaysian Industrial Development Finance Limited (MIDFL), The Pakistan Industrial Credit and Investment Corporation Limited (PICIC), the Private Development Corporation of the Philippines (PDCP), and the Industrial Finance Corporation of Thailand (IFCT). A brief analysis of each IFC commitment follows in this section.

Pakistan Industrial Credit and Investment Corporation Limited (PICIC)

The first IFC assistance to a development finance company in this area took place during IFC's 1962-1963 fiscal year. IFC subscribed to 200,000 common PICIC shares at 107 per cent of their par value of 10 rupees per share, or a total of $449,400.

PICIC is the principal private institution furnishing medium- and long-term financing to industrial firms in Pakistan. The company was organized in 1957

by Pakistani and foreign investors including the
World Bank, which took an important role in PICIC's
organization.   PICIC was organized with resources
which included a thirty-year interest-free advance
of 30 million rupees ($6.1 million), with a fifteen-
year grace period, from the Pakistani government.
By February, 1963, the World Bank had made loans
totaling $50 million to PICIC.   Sixty per cent of
PICIC's stock is held by Pakistani investors and
the remainder is held by British (10.8 per cent),
German (6 per cent), Japanese (7.3 per cent), and
American (10.9 per cent) investors as well as IFC,
which held 5 per cent of PICIC's shares as of
December 31, 1966.

PICIC's operations are similar to those of IFC.
In addition to financing industrial operations,
PICIC underwrites public share offerings and helps
Pakistani firms to find managerial, technical and
administrative services.   At the time of the IFC
commitment to PICIC, the latter had approved over
300 loans totaling over $84 million, held stock in
local firms amounting to $2,960,000, had under-
written shares totaling $3,200,000, and helped find
$10 million of foreign capital for Pakistani firms.[15]

PICIC attempted to broaden shareownership in
Pakistan by considering as a prerequisite to
granting a loan to an applicant, the requirement
that a closely held applicant company issue shares
to the public.   However, the Pakistani government
diluted this attempted resolution by decreeing that
60 per cent of all new capital issues by existing
or newly formed companies be offered to the public.[16]

Private Development Corporation
of the Philippines (PDCP)

The World Bank and IFC helped to organize PDCP
in February, 1963, as a development finance company
whose functions are similar to those of IFC except
operations are on a local basis.   PDCP makes medium-
and long-term loans to Philippine firms, invests in
the equity of companies, underwrites new issues,

and provides managerial and technical advice.[17]
Between 1963 and 1966, PDCP made investment in
fifteen different industries.

PDCP was formed with 500,000 shares of Class A
stock subscribed to by local sponsors. In June,
1963, PDCP offered its remaining authorized
1,250,000 Class A shares. An offering of 750,000
Class B shares was also made. IFC subscribed to
500,000 Class A shares, agreeing to take 80,000
initially and the remainder on a standby basis if
the public offering was unsuccessful. IFC was re-
lieved of its standby commitment because of the
success of the offering. However, payment for the
subscriptions was slow. Therefore, IFC agreed to
pay defaulted balances up to 14,520,000 pesos
(approximately $3.72 million) in return for the
unpaid shares. Thus, the total IFC commitment
amounted to the equivalent of a standby arrangement
of $4,359,063.

PDCP's Class B shares were subscribed to by
eighteen leading financial institutions outside the
Philippines. These are listed in Table 11. In
addition, the World Bank loaned PDCP $15 million
and the U.S. Agency for International Development
also made a loan.

Since the share issue in 1963 by PDCP, the
shares increased in value on the Manila market from
10 to 14 pesos. During 1967, IFC sold its holdings
at the latter price to Philippine institutional
investors, thus making a good profit.

PDCP has benefited the Philippine economy by
its four underwritings and by its investments in
industries such as transportation, power, food,
textiles, wood and cork, printing and publishing,
chemicals, glass, clay and stone products, basic
metal products, machinery, electrical machinery,
and mining.[18]

In addition, PDCP has established working relationships with other Philippine financial institutions in assisting in public issue underwritings.
A separate subsidiary has been initiated by PDCP to

Table 11

Foreign Financial Institutions
Investing in PDCP Shares

1. The American Express Company, Inc.
2. Bank of America N.T. & S.A.
3. The Bank of Tokyo, Ltd
4. Bankers International Financing
   Company, Inc.
5. Boston Overseas Financial Corporation
6. The Chartered Bank
7. Chemical International Finance Ltd.
8. Continental International Finance
   Corporation
9. Deutsche Bank A.G.
10. First National City Overseas
    Investment Corporation
11. The Hong Kong and Shanghai Banking
    Corporation
12. Irving International Financing
    Corporation
13. Lehman Brothers
14. Manufacturers Hanover International
    Finance Corporation
15. Morgan Guaranty International
    Finance Corporation
16. New York Hanseatic Corporation
17. Philadelphia International Investment
    Corporation
18. Wells Fargo Bank International
    Corporation

Source: IFC, <u>Seventh Annual Report 1962-1963</u>
(Washington, D.C.: International Finance
Corporation, 1963), p. 21.

121

use the facilities of firms, such as insurance companies, which have widespread business coverage to
implement this activity.[19]

Malaysian Industrial Development
Finance Limited (MIDFL)

IFC teamed with the World Bank in July, 1963,
to increase the equity base and financial resources
of MIDFL so that this development finance company
might increase its activities in industrial development in Malaysia. Malaysian investors and private
foreign financial interests participated in the investment.

MIDFL's total equity capital was increased
from 17.5 million Malayan dollars to M$25 million
(about U.S. $8 million). The World Bank loaned
MIDFL M$25 million in foreign exchange and the
Government of Malaysia made a thirty-year, interest-
free loan of M$37.5 million. Thus MIDFL's resources
were increased to the equivalent of U.S. $28.6
million.[20]

New shares in MIDFL were issued totaling M$7.5
million. The company's shares were already held by
many foreign financial institutions including French,
Chinese, Indian, Japanese, Thai, British, and American banks. Two American banks, Bankers International Financing Company and Manufacturers Hanover
International Finance Corporation, and one German
bank, Deutsche Bank A.G., became new investors in
MIDFL by buying shares of the new issue. Presently,
Malaysian private investors, the Malaysian Central
Bank, and the local Ministry of Finance hold about
40 per cent of MIDFL's shares. The remainder is
held by IFC and private foreign investors.

IFC's commitment was to purchase shares
amounting to the U.S. equivalent of $817,917 and to
agree to a standby to purchase shares totaling up
to U.S. $490,000. Thus, the total commitment was
for U.S. $1,307,917.

MIDFL agreed in 1963, as a condition for obtaining a government loan, to make up to 20 per cent of its annual commitments in amounts of $17,000 to $50,000 to small business enterprises. This business was not as voluminous as the government expected because only 4 per cent, 5 per cent, and 8 per cent of total investments for 1964, 1965, and 1966, respectively, were for amounts less than $50,000. Ordinary long-term loans were more profitable than the smaller loans, made primarily for rental agreements and factory mortgages.[21]

Industrial Finance Corporation of Thailand (IFCT)

IFCT is the leading private development financial institution in Thailand offering both loan and share capital to industrial firms of a rapidly expanding economy. In March, 1964, IFCT's financial resources were expanded by a new equity issue subscribed to by IFC and Thai and foreign investors, and by loans received from the World Bank and the Kreditanstalt für Wiederaufbau of Frankfurt, Germany.

A 30 million baht (approximately $1.5 million) share issue was made and IFC subscribed to 4 million baht ($193,108). Thai investors took 13.9 million baht and the remainder was purchased by a number of foreign financial institutions including Bank of America, The Bank of Tokyo, Commerzbank A.G., Mitsui Bank Limited, and Wells Fargo Bank International Corporation.[22]

The loans amounted to 109.2 million baht (over $5 million) and consisted of 57.2 million baht from the German development bank and 52 million baht from the World Bank. IFCT has subordinated debt owed to the Thai government of 48.1 million baht. These investments increased IFCT's financial resources to 187.3 million baht (approximately $9 million).

Thai investors--mainly banking and insurance institutions--hold 46 per cent of IFCT's expanded share capital, IFC holds 13 per cent, and foreign financial institutions hold the remainder.

Summary

IFC has made four investments in private development finance companies in the Asian-Middle East area. These consisted of operational investments in the four institutions amounting to $1,460,425 and standby agreements amounting to $4,849,063. The total commitments amounted to $6,309,488. The institutions in Malaysia, the Philippines, and Thailand have financial resources totaling over $66 million and PICIC's commitments alone by 1962 had totaled well over that amount. Thus, IFC has successfully implemented one of its principal objectives in assisting the expansion of these financial institutions whose operations will expand IFC's aid to local enterprise much in the same manner as IFC itself operates internationally.

CHAPTER 7 THE INTERNATIONAL
FINANCE CORPORATION
IN AFRICA

INTRODUCTION

During the early years of IFC operations,
emphasis was placed on investments in business
firms located in Latin America. However, during
the 1960's, many African countries have gained
their independence and new states have been formed.
The entire continent, with the exception of the
Union of South Africa and a very few specific regions, is in a state of relatively extreme underdevelopment. Such is especially true of private
enterprise in Africa. Entrepreneurial activity
has been greatly centralized and is weak in nature.
Administrators in Africa with managerial skills
are few in number. Because of these problems, the
supply of venture capital for private enterprise
has been low in this area of the world.

The World Bank Group began to recognize these
problems early in this decade. The World Bank itself first made a commitment in Africa in 1950.
However, IFC did not make an investment there until
1960 when a rather large commitment was made in the
Kilombero Sugar Company of Tanzania (then Tanganyika).[1]
The World Bank appointed a Special Representative
for Africa in 1961. A separate department dealing
in African development was formed in 1962 and a
study by the Special Representative, taking two
years, was completed in 1963. The International
Development Association made its first credits in

Africa in 1961.[2] Thus, the World Bank Group has
been quite active in Africa since 1960.

Since making a commitment to the Kilombero
Sugar Company in 1960, IFC has made an additional
thirteen investments in Africa by the end of the
1966 fiscal year of operations. The fourteen commitments totaled $22,914,192, as shown in Table 12,
and were made in nine of the African nations.[3]

IFC commitments in Africa have been made to
both industrial firms and private development finance companies. Of the fourteen investments, nine
were made in eight industrial firms. Commitments
were made to five private development finance companies. These specific investments are listed in
Table 13.

Table 12

IFC Investment, Standby and
Underwriting Commitments, 1956-1966,
Africa

Country	Initial Commitment	No. of Commitments	Funds Committed
Ethiopia	1964	2	$ 4,407,557
Ivory Coast	1965	1	204,081
Liberia	1965	1	250,000
Morocco	1963	2	2,880,993
Nigeria	1963	2	2,169,801
Sudan	1964	1	688,893
Tanzania	1960	2	4,731,085
Tunisia	1962	2	4,071,428
Uganda	1965	1	3,510,354
Totals		14	$22,914,192

Source: IFC, Annual Report 1965-1966 (Washington,
         D.C.: International Finance Corporation,
         1966), p. 4.

The following sections of this chapter will
consist of detailed case analyses of five IFC commitments in industrial firms. These are the Cotton
Company of Ethiopia, the Kilombero Sugar Company of
Tanzania, Mulco Textiles, Limited, of Uganda, NPK-
Engrais, **S.A.T.** of Tunisia, and **Arewa** Textiles of
Nigeria. In addition, the five IFC investments in
development finance companies will be briefly discussed.

Among the criteria used for selecting these
five industrial firms for analysis were the magnitude of the investments, the need for increasing
production of the companies' products, the benefits
accruing to the countries from each company, and
other unique experiences which have occurred after
the investment commitments were made.

KILOMBERO SUGAR COMPANY, LTD.

Tanzania is a country formed by a merger of
the former countries of Tanganyika and Zanzibar in
1964. Tanganyika gained independence in 1961 and
became a republic one year later. Before these
incidents, Tanganyika was a United Nations Trust
Territory administered by the United Kingdom. A
little larger than Pakistan, it is a nation with an
area of over 360,000 square miles and a population
of 10 million including over 80,000 Asians, 20,000
Arabs, and 20,000 Europeans.

The economy is primarily agricultural. The
principal products and exports are sisal, coffee,
cotton, and cloves. Most of the agricultural output is for subsistence and the industrial sector
in 1960 contributed only 6 per cent to total gross
national product.

An informal customs union including Tanganyika,
Kenya, and Uganda linked the economies of these
countries during the late 1950's and early 1960's.
Plans were to eventually formalize this arrangement.
However, Tanganyika has remained a very relatively
underdeveloped area.

Table 13

IFC Commitments in Africa by Company

Company	Country	Operational Investment	Standby and Underwriting
Cotton Company of Ethiopia, S.C.	Ethiopia	$ 2,507,557	$ ---
Ethiopian Pulp and Paper, S.C.	"	200,000	1,700,000
Banque Ivoirienne de Développement Industriel, S.A.	Ivory Coast	204,081	---
Liberian Bank for Industrial Development and Investment	Liberia	---	250,000
Banque Nationale pour le Développement Economique	Morocco	1,495,774	---
Compañia Industrial del Lukus, S.A.	"	1,385,219	---
Nigerian Industrial Development Bank Limited	Nigeria	---	1,400,000
Arewa Textiles, Ltd.	"	769,801	---

Khartoum Spinning and Weaving Company, Ltd.	Sudan	688,893	---
Kilombero Sugar Company, Ltd.	Tanzania	4,731,085	---
NPK-Engrais, S.A.T.	Tunisia	3,500,000	---
Société Nationale d'Investissement	"	571,428	---
Mulco Textiles, Ltd.	Uganda	3,510,354	---
Totals		$ 19,564,192	$ 3,350,000

Source: IFC, Annual Report 1965-1966 (Washington, D.C.: International Finance Corporation, 1966), Appendix C, pp. 34, 36, and 38.

Tanganyika had been an importer of sugar for many years prior to 1960. Although per capita sugar consumption was low in Tanganyika--about one third that of Kenya in 1959[4]--nevertheless, scarce foreign exchange was needed for the importation of sugar. A project leading to development of the Kilombero Valley in Tanganyika was proposed. One of the industrial enterprises proposed in this development plan was a new manufacturing company, Kilombero Sugar Company, Limited (KSC), which would grow and mill sugar cane and produce sugar for the Tanganyikan market. This enterprise would distribute sugar more effectively than the import business so that local consumption would be increased and, at the same time, foreign exchange reserves would not be needed for purchase of sugar. Total cost of this project was estimated at over $8 million.[5]

KSC had acquired a land concession from the government on the Great Ruaha River in the Kilombero Valley. About 7,000 acres were to be cleared for sugar cane and a sugar mill with a capacity of 20,000 tons was to be erected. Expansion to 30,000 tons capacity was planned with production to begin in 1962.

IFC, together with the Colonial Development Corporation (CDC), the Netherlands Overseas Finance Company (NOFC), and Vereenigde Klattensche Cultuur Maatschappij (VKCM), committed $6.4 million. This was IFC's first commitment in Africa. The remaining portion of the project cost consisted of an issue totaling nearly $2 million of convertible preferred shares issued by KSC and subscribed by the Standard Bank of South Africa and CDC, and a supplier's credit of £210,000. The convertible preferred stock was offered for sale to Africans and other Tanganyikan residents. IFC's total commitment was the equivalent of $2,800,000. The financing is as follows:[6]

1.   £1,150,000 debentures carrying
7 per cent interest, maturing between
1967 and 1973.   These include $1.4
million and £250,000 subscribed by IFC,
£300,000 subscribed by CDC, and 1,060,000
Dutch guilders subscribed by NOFC;

2.   £500,000 convertible income notes
maturing between 1973 and 1975, subscribed
in equal amounts by IFC and CDC, and
carrying a return contingent on earnings
but no interest;

3.   £650,000 ordinary share capital--
£250,000 subscribed by CDC, £270,000
by NOFC, and £130,000 by VKCM;

4.   IFC, CDC, and NOFC received
ordinary shares or options as a
commission for subscribing to the
debentures.

The operations of KSC were to be managed by
VKCM.   A labor force of 4,000 was planned at that
time and the project included housing for workers
as well as medical and welfare facilities for KSC
personnel.

Production began in 1962-1963 and 11,000 tons
of sugar were produced.   However, the company incurred a net loss of more than £250,000 ($700,000).
Production for the second season was forecast to be
21,000 tons but production realized only 12,700 tons
because of an unforeseen shortage of mature cane.
Further losses resulted and the need for new funds
became very apparent.

An investigation was initiated by the three
principal shareowners.   A group of sugar experts
determined that KSC's potential was great and that
the expansion to 31,500 tons capacity should be
implemented.   Recommendations about management,
organization, and agricultural practices were also
made.

KFC, CDC, and NOFC decided in 1964 to reorganize the capital structure of the company. New funds were to be provided and new management and technical expertise were injected into KSC.

The new financial arrangements were as follows:

    1.   The convertible income notes held by IFC, CDC, and NOFC were converted into ordinary shares;

    2.   The convertible cumulative preferred stock, except for that held by Tanganyikans, was converted into ordinary shares;

    3.   The debentures were converted into income notes with extended maturities and accrued and unpaid interest was cancelled;

    4.   An initial investment was made by the three investment institutions in senior debentures totaling £1,500,000 ($4.2 million) to replenish working capital and provide for expansion.

The IFC share in the new financial structure consisted of £690,000 in debentures ($1,931,172), £750,000 in income notes, and £325,000 in ordinary shares including £75,000 at no cost. The total new infusion of capital, $4.2 million, brought total investment in KSC to $13.9 million. The new IFC commitment totaled $1,931,172, bringing IFC's total commitments in KSC to $4,731,172.

Losses continued to occur at Kilombero Sugar Company. Through the 1965-1966 fiscal year, KSC had accumulated losses of 7,728,637 shillings ($21,640,000) although 1965-1966 operations resulted in a profit of 1,179,710 shillings. Production of refined sugar in 1965-1966 totaled 24,813 long tons compared with 20,497 long tons in 1964-1965.[7]

Adverse weather during the 1965-1966 operating year resulted in a low sucrose content. As a result of this, and yellow wilt disease (a disease found nowhere else in the world) the outlook for a profitable 1966-1967 operating year was considered poor. Increased wages, salaries, cost of goods, and taxes during the year have added to the bleakness of the current outlook. However, full capacity of 31,500 tons was reached during 1967.[8] Tanzania has now become self-sufficient in sugar although per capita consumption is lower relatively than in neighboring nations.

The near-term outlook at KSC is bleak. However, the weather has contributed greatly to the problems incurred by the company. The area seems to be in the last stages of a seven-year drought cycle. This caused unforeseen higher irrigation costs. As technical expertise matures and the disease and cost problems are alleviated, profitability should improve so that good weather years could result in large gains for KSC. The long-term prospects seem to be good and another enterprise is becoming established in a developing nation as a result of IFC operations. The entire Kilombero Valley development project was a very ambitious undertaking. Coupled with this, the Kilombero Sugar Company was the boldest-type investment. However, counting the sugar growers, 20,000 people are now employed in the area and new villages are being built in the valley.

NPK-ENGRAIS, S.A.T.

Tunisia, with a population of approximately 4.5 million and an area of 48,000 square miles, is the smallest North African nation. Independent since 1956, Tunisia has a large tourism potential because of its Mediterranean coastline. The country has large deposits of iron ore, lead, and phosphates and although half its area is desert, much of the remaining area is very fertile. About one fourth of the contribution to gross national product comes from the agricultural sector. The per capita national income in 1966 was about $200.

The World Bank Group began activities in Tunisia in 1962 when the International Development Association extended a $5 million credit for secondary and technical school construction.[9]

During 1962, a leading Swedish producer of fertilizers, Aktiebolaget Forenade Superfosfat-fabriker (Forenade) of Helsingborg, Sweden, decided to sponsor a new Tunisian company which would manufacture triple superphosphate fertilizers. The new plant was located at the Port of Sfax on the Gulf of Gabes, about 150 miles south of Tunis. The plant, designed to produce 150,000 tons annually, was built next to docking facilities at Sfax, a terminal for a railway from interior rock phosphate mines. The city is the leading port for shipments of Tunisian phosphate.[10] The plant, designed by Forenade, was intended to be used twenty-four hours a day for eleven months annually.

Forenade applied for financial assistance from IFC. An IFC study resulted in a few significant changes in the original proposal. First, IFC proposed that the new company build its own sulphuric acid plant using imported sulphur, instead of importing the finished product, thus giving the new company a cost advantage. Forenade agreed and IFC persuaded Freeport International Inc., a financial investment subsidiary of a leading American sulphur producer, to participate in the investment.[11] Secondly, IFC suggested that Forenade arrange to sell the bulk of NPK's output to Swedish purchasers on a long-term basis. The remainder would be exported to African and Asian countries. Thus, sale of NPK's output would be assured.[12]

The appraisal by IFC resulted in increased project costs. The total initial cost of NPK was $14.2 million. IFC agreed to make its first commitment in North Africa by investing $1.5 million in NPK shares and lending $2 million at 7 per cent for 7 years. Forenade agreed to purchase $3.5 million NPK shares and to lend the company $2,150,000. Freeport International bought $1 million of shares and made a $600,000 loan to the project. A unique

feature of the financial arrangements was that each
of these three investors agreed to reserve one-
tenth of its NPK stock for sale to private Tunisian
investors at par.[13] The remaining portion of the
capital needs was obtained through suppliers' credits and other loan sources.

As usual, IFC sought outside financial participation. Approximately $1 million of IFC's loan
and share commitments were taken by American and
foreign financial institutions. Laidlaw Securities
Limited of Canada, a subsidiary of Laidlaw and
Company of New York, subscribed to $154,000 of IFC's
share commitment in NPK. Algemene Commerciele
Associatie N.V., a Dutch banking house affiliated
with Hambros Bank of London, subscribed to $100,000
of the NPK shares held by IFC. New World Development Corporation Limited, an affiliate of the
Philadelphia National Bank, took $100,000 of the
shares and $286,000 of the IFC loan commitment to
NPK. Bank of America N.T. & S.A. and Svenska Handelsbanken, a Swedish bank, took equal parts totaling $286,000 of the IFC loan commitment to NPK.[14]

The company began operations in 1964, almost a
year ahead of the original schedule. The plant
should contribute economically to Tunisia by expanding the use of an important Tunisian natural
resource and the exports of superphosphate fertilizers should contribute to Tunisian foreign exchange
reserves. In addition to these possible results,
nearly 400 Tunisians have been employed by the new
enterprise and a technical training program is
being maintained by NPK to advance the technical,
administrative, and managerial skills of the employees. Finally, local investors are beginning to
buy NPK shares in order to participate in the new
enterprise.

Although these advantages may accrue to the
Tunisian economy, there has been some indication
that this enterprise is lacking the market potential which could make exporting successful.[15]
Since exporting is a significant part of NPK's output, this venture may incur some serious problems
in the near future.

COTTON COMPANY OF ETHIOPIA

Ethiopia, located in Eastern Africa, is a kingdom over 3,000 years old, whose capital is Addis Ababa. The country comprises an area of nearly 400,000 square miles and a population estimated to be nearly 25 million. Agriculture accounts for the vast bulk of the economy of Ethiopia, making up nearly 90 per cent of economic production. The present Emperor, Haile Selassie I, was crowned in 1930.

Ethiopia is predominately an agricultural nation and, therefore, a relatively underdeveloped country. The largest single import item in 1964 was finished textiles. The Cotton Company of Ethiopia, S.C., leading producer of textiles, had a small mill located at Dire Dawa. A majority interest in the firm had been acquired in 1963 by two well-known Japanese companies, Fuji Spinning Company Limited and Marubeni-Iida Company Limited.

During 1964, the company decided to initiate a $5,410,000 expansion program including modernization of the Dire Dawa plant, expansion of its finishing facilities, and construction of a new plant adjacent to its existing plant. The new plant was equipped with 12,000 spindles and 400 looms. This project was designed to satisfy rising demand in Ethiopia for higher quality textiles as well as to meet competition from local producers and imports.

An application for financial assistance was made to IFC which agreed to invest $2,507,557 in the project by making a loan of $1.5 million to Cotton Company and purchasing shares in the firm equivalent to $1,007,557. The two Japanese companies invested the equivalent of $1,650,000 and the Export-Import Bank of Japan made a loan for the remaining portion of the project's financial cost to cover a portion of purchases of machinery and equipment.[16]

IFC also encouraged private foreign financial
institutions to participate in the project. The
Bamerical International Financial Corporation, a
Bank of America subsidiary, and the Irving Trust
Company participated in the IFC loan to the extent
of $430,000.[17]

In addition to these financial arrangements,
the two Japanese companies began providing managerial and technical staff to Cotton Company early in
1964. A training program for Ethiopian staff, in
both Ethiopia and Japan, was initiated in 1964.
Two Ethiopian technicians are now being trained in
Japan each year by the Fuji Management Group.

The new plant at Dire Dawa did not go on stream
until October, 1966. However, by May 31, 1967, the
end of Cotton Company's fiscal year, the increased
capacity had resulted in a number of benefits to
the company and its owners. Increased productivity
and efficiency, resulting in a higher quality product, were possible because of the expansion. Net
profits after taxes increased from Ethiopian
$255,062 in FY 1966 to Ethiopian $2,719,377 in FY
1967. Finished goods inventories, very high in
1966, were reduced by nearly 50 per cent in 1967.[18]

Further benefits are accruing to Ethiopia as a
result of this project. Foreign exchange reserves
are being saved by using locally grown cotton as a
raw material and by selling the firm's output on
the local market.[19] More than 60 per cent of the
raw cotton was locally grown during fiscal year
1967.[20]

MULCO TEXTILES LIMITED OF UGANDA

Uganda is located in eastern Africa between
Kenya to the east, Sudan in the north, the Republic
of the Congo in the west, and Rwanda and Tanzania
in the south. Uganda's area consists of 93,981
square miles. The population of Uganda is more than
7.5 million.[21] The nation gained its independence
from British rule in 1962 and became a republic in
1963.

Uganda's economy is primarily peasant agriculture. Coffee and cotton are the principal cash crops. Tea is also grown and the lakes furnish large amounts of fish. There is copper mining in western Uganda. The nation has loose economic ties with Kenya and Tanzania and is part of the proposed three nation common market area.

During 1965, a new company, Mulco Textiles Limited, was formed to build a fully integrated cotton textile mill at Jinja, a town near Lake Victoria. This mill, using Ugandan cotton, was equipped with 24,220 spindles and 450 looms. Finishing equipment for bleaching and dyeing was also included. Full capacity of 18 million square yards of cloth, mainly gray cloth and piece dyed material, was planned.[22]

Local sponsors included two well-known companies in East Africa, the Madhvani Sugar Works Limited, largest sugar maker in East Africa, and Muljibhai Madhvani and Company Limited, a holding company composed of trading branches and interests in the steel, glass, brewing, and match industries.

This group and other local investors financed the majority of the project's total estimated cost of $7,728,000. The Madhvani group invested $2,312,800 in share capital and private Ugandan investors subscribed shares totaling $123,200. The equivalent of $1,848,000 was borrowed by Mulco in the short-term money market.

The remaining portion of the investment was committed by IFC. A loan of $2,800,000 was made by IFC, as well as a share investment amounting to $644,000. Two English financial institutions as well as one located in Kuwait participated to the extent of $1,292,000 in the IFC commitment. The Standard Bank Finance and Development Corporation, an affiliate of The Standard Bank Limited of London, participated to the extent of $980,000. Of this amount, $140,000 was for share capital. Barclays Overseas Development Corporation, a subsidiary of Barclays D.C.O. of London, contributed $172,000

toward the IFC share, including $32,000 for stock
capital. Finally, the Kuwait Investment Company
participated in the IFC portion in the amount of
$140,000. IFC also made a standby commitment for
shares totaling $70,000.[23]

The sales of Mulco were expected to benefit
from the trade policies of the East African Common
Market of Kenya, Tanzania, and Uganda. Free trade
in textiles was to be allowed in this area. All of
Mulco's output was planned to be sold in this area
where a market exists of more than 25 million. The
company's production will assist conservation of
Ugandan foreign exchange reserves by satisfying
local demand for textiles which has normally been
satisfied by imports. Local consumption has been
rising by 5 per cent annually and is estimated to
be more than 260 million square yards by 1970.[24]

However, Mulco was caught in the middle of the
breakup of the East African Common Market. The
three countries closed their markets to the others'
textile products. Nita, a Ugandan producer of 60
million square yards of textiles annually, and Mulco,
producing 6 million square yards, were both hurt by
the political situation. The larger company lowered
its prices but Mulco stubbornly met Nita's prices
to remain competitive.

Government officials began repairing the breakdown among the East African countries, and finally,
early in 1967, an agreement was signed whereby Tanzania agreed to take 250,000 square yards of Mulco's
output. By December, 1967, the Common Market was
reformed with guaranteed markets for Ugandan textile
producers, including Mulco. On December 1, 1967,
the East African Economic and Social Community,
linking Uganda, Kenya, and Tanzania, was initiated.
This is to be a cooperative agreement "embracing
everything from a regional common market and development bank to fisheries research and higher education."[25] Other nations, including Zambia, Ethiopia,
and Somalia, have expressed desire to enter the
agreement.[26]

The agreement was formalized by the Treaty of East African Co-operation which calls for the free movement of goods between the three countries. However, import licensing in Uganda will continue for statistical purposes. In addition, transfer taxes have been imposed by the treaty. A tax agreement allows member countries to impose the tax--in essence, a tariff--if the nation imports more manufactured goods than it sells to a neighboring state. The nations of the treaty agreement have imposed the tax on a number of goods including spirits, paints, blankets, aluminum, footwear, brooms, and textiles. Tanzania has imposed a transfer tax on Ugandan textiles including unprinted woven cotton fabrics.[28]

It is too early to estimate the effect of the new agreement or the transfer tax imposition on Mulco's production. Until this political situation has been alleviated and fully defined, Mulco will probably remain in trouble. No one could have foreseen these events when Mulco was first proposed by its sponsors. Mulco's future success will depend very much on the East African governments.[29]

AREWA TEXTILES LIMITED OF NIGERIA

The Federation of Nigeria, located on the west coast of Africa, has an area of 356,668 square miles and a population of 57.5 million. The nation is bordered by Niger on the north and northwest, Lake Chad on the northeast, Cameroun on the east, the Gulf of Guinea on the south, and Dahomey on the west. The major ethnic groups are the Yoruba and Ibo in the south and the Hausa and the Arab-like Fulani in the north. Nigeria's economy is dependent on primary raw materials such as agricultural, forest, and mineral. Health standards are low and most tropical diseases are prevalent.[30]

The political situation in Nigeria has been one of violent turmoil since 1965. Elections in 1965 led to bloody reprisals and a military coup in early 1966. Top government officials were

assassinated and part of the country revolted during
1967 to form the new government of Biafra.

One of Nigeria's major agricultural products
for export is cotton. However, before 1964, Nigeria
also imported large amounts of cotton cloth and
other textiles. Thus, an integrated textile industry had a built-in base for development.

In March, 1964, IFC joined with a group of ten
leading Japanese cotton textile firms and two Nigerian development institutions to finance the construction of an integrated cotton textile mill at
Kaduna, in the Northern Region, by Arewa Textiles
Limited, a new company.

The Japanese group, the Overseas Spinning Investment Company Limited (OSIC), was established
for the purpose of investing in textile projects
outside Japan and providing them with managerial
and technical advice. The two Nigerian institutions
were the Northern Nigeria Development Corporation
and Northern Nigeria Investments Limited.

The total cost of the project was $4.48 million.
The two Nigerian financing institutions contributed
long-term financing of approximately $980,000. Of
the total 1.6 million Nigerian pounds cost of the
investment, OSIC contributed £N420,000 in shares,
or 60 per cent of Arewa's equity, and £N480,000 for
machinery credits. OSIC also agreed to recruit
Japanese for management and technical assistance.[31]

IFC contributed the remainder of the capital,
$770,078, consisting of £N117,000 for capital shares,
£133,000 (sterling) in loans, and £N25,000 standby
credit in the event of cost overruns.[32] In addition, Barclays Overseas Development Corporation
Limited, London, a subsidiary of Barclays D.C.O.,
Handelsfinanz A.G., Zurich, and the Kuwait Investment Company agreed to participate in IFC's loans.
In order to encourage local investment, IFC and the
Nigerian institutions reserved 10 per cent of their
holdings for sale to Nigerian investors.

The Arewa investment is unusual for a number of reasons. It was IFC's first commitment in Nigeria and the first in which IFC cooperated with Japanese industrial interests. OSIC overcame all the problems inherent in a tribal situation in training the Hausa. The Japanese utilized the latest managerial and technical skills, including marketing research, and thereby achieved a three-shift operation within three to four months. The company went on stream in late 1965, a full year ahead of schedule, and reported a profit after the first year of operations.[33] By 1967, Arewa had exceeded original production targets by 20 per cent and was producing 12 million yards of cloth annually. Plans were made to triple this output to 36 million yards by 1968 by means of an additional $5 million expansion project to which IFC contributed $831,324 in additional share and loan capital.[34]

With this mill, Nigeria can now satisfy half its needs for cotton fabric. Arewa will consume 9 per cent of the Nigerian cotton crop after this expansion and employ over 1,650 Nigerian staff.[35] In addition, Arewa declared its first dividend in fiscal 1967, very early for a new company.[36]

Arewa was able to accomplish its objectives in much less time than originally planned in spite of the Nigerian civil war. Production has not been affected by the political problems. Without the cooperation of the Nigerian government, IFC assistance, and the Japanese expertise, the successful results of Arewa probably would not have occurred.

IFC COMMITMENTS TO AFRICAN DEVELOPMENT FINANCE COMPANIES

IFC has made investment commitments in five private development finance companies in Africa. The first of these was in 1963 when an operational investment was made in Banque Nationale pour le Développement Economique of Morocco. The other investments were in the Nigerian Industrial Development Bank, Limited; the Liberian Bank for Industrial

Development and Investment; Banque Ivoirienne de
Développement Industriel, S.A. of Ivory Coast; and
Société Nationale d'Investissement of Tunisia. A
total of $2,271,283 in operational investments and
$1,650,000 in standby and underwriting commitments
have been made by IFC in African development finance companies, for a total of $3,921,283.

Banque Nationale pour le Développement
Economique (BNDE) of Morocco

In 1963, IFC joined with the World Bank for
the first time in financing a private development
finance company. IFC subscribed to shares in BNDE
amounting to $1.5 million and the World Bank made a
$15 million loan.[37]

Established by the Moroccan government in 1959,
BNDE had made direct loans totaling $12.6 million
during the period 1959-1962. The IFC investment of
$1,485,692 in shares was part of an expansion of
the share capital of BNDE from $4 million to $6 million. The Moroccan government and Morgan Guaranty
International Finance Corporation of New York subscribed to the remaining shares.

Other shareholders in BNDE include: French
financial institutions such as Caisse de Dépôts et
Consignations and Caisse Centrale de Cooperation
Economique; Italian banks such as Banca Nazionale
del Lavoro, Istituto Mobiliare Italiano and Banca
Commerciale Italiana; German banks such as Deutsche
Bank, Dresdner Bank, Commerzbank, and Westfalenbank;
and Banque Lambert, a Belgian bank.[38]

Nigerian Industrial Development
Bank Limited (NIDB)

IFC assisted in the complex negotiations which
led to establishment of NIDB, an outgrowth of the
Investment Company of Nigeria Limited (ICON), in
1964. Leading American, European, and Japanese investment institutions participated in the formation
of this private development finance company.

The initial total capital of NIDB amounted to
$11.9 million including a long-term, interest-free
loan of $5.6 million from the Federal Republic of
Nigeria.[39] A total of $6.3 million share capital
was issued. This included $2,856,000 Class A ordi-
nary shares subscribed to by the Central Bank of
Nigeria, Nigerian private investors, and IFC. The
IFC subscription was for $1,400,000. Former ICON
owners subscribed to 51 per cent of the $2,744,000
Class B ordinary shares and to all of the $700,000
issue of preferred stock in NIDB.

Among the foreign institutions subscribing to
the Class B ordinary shares were Chase International
Investment Corporation, Istituto Mobiliare Italiano,
Bank of America, The Bank of Tokyo, Commerzbank of
Germany, and Société Financière pour les Pays
d'Outre-Mer S.A. of France.[40] IFC and the Nigerian
Central Bank agreed to sell their shares to local
investors when possible.

One of the significant activities of NIDB has
been its encouragement of new foreign companies in
Nigeria to offer their shares for sale to the public
and to list these securities on the Lagos Stock Exchange. This has been facilitated by ICON Securities, a wholly owned subsidiary of NIDB. ICON also
maintains a pool of securities that it can trade
for its own account. Such trading aids the small
investor in a thin market such as that which pre-
vails in Nigeria. Better maintenance of securities
prices has been accomplished in this manner.[41]

Banque Ivoirienne de Développement Industriel, S.A. (BIDI) of Ivory Coast

BIDI was formed in early 1965 and, at the request of the Ivory Coast government, was sponsored
by Chase International Investment Corporation and
Lazard Frères & Company, both of New York. The
company was formed for the purpose of operating as
a private development finance company.

BIDI began operations with total resources of
$12.9 million including a $5 million interest-free,
long-term loan from the Ivory Coast government and
a $5 million credit from the U.S. Agency for Inter-
national Development. This latter credit was made
for the purpose of relending to local businesses.

Share capital represented the remaining $2.9
million of initial resources. This was divided
equally between Class A and B shares. IFC, making
its first commitment in Ivory Coast, subscribed to
Class A shares in an amount equivalent to $204,081.
African and French governmental agencies and the
Ivory Coast government subscribed to the remaining
Class A shares. Private foreign and Ivorian investors subscribed to the Class B shares.[42]

Liberian Bank for Industrial Development and Investment (LBIDI)

IFC made its first investment in Liberia in
1965 when it participated in the formation of a new
private development finance company, the Liberian
Bank for Industrial Development and Investment (LBIDI).
The new company was formed with $4.5 million total
resources of which $1 million represented share
capital subscribed to in the following amounts:

1.	Private foreign investors	$ 490,000
2.	Liberian investors	260,000
3.	IFC	250,000
	Total	$1,000,000

A loan of $2.5 million was made by the Kreditanstalt
für Wiederaufbau of Germany, and the Liberian government loaned LBIDI $1 million.

Besides the IFC share investment other local
and foreign investors participated by making share
subscriptions. Among these were the Liberian Development Corporation; Bank of Monrovia, an affiliate
of First National City Bank of New York; Firestone
Plantations Company, International Trust Company of
Liberia; Istituto Mobiliare Italiano; LAMCO Joint

Venture; and Liberia Mining Company Limited.[43] The
Liberian Development Corporation is a government-
owned agency and, although it was desired that the
Liberian investors all be from the private sector,
this government agency subscribed to $250,000 in
shares. Thus, private investors purchased only
$10,000 of the stock.[44] In addition, the U.S.
Agency for International Development is assisting
LBIDI by offering the services of a U.S. management
consultant company for investigating project proposals as well as aiding in the initial cost of
LBIDI's management.[45] IFC, in keeping with its objectives, agreed to reserve its shares in LBIDI for
purchase by private Liberian investors as a means
of broadening local ownership in the company.

Société Nationale d'Investissement of Tunisia (SNI)

SNI is a development finance company established in 1959. In 1966, IFC and the World Bank
joined with the Tunisian government and other local
and European investors in the expansion of SNI's
total resources.

The expansion plan called for a reorganization
of SNI so that its previous emphasis in the government sector would be replaced with the objective of
primarily financing the private sector as a private
development finance company. Private ownership replaced governmental control.

Among the additional capital resources were a
$5 million World Bank loan and IFC's commitment to
subscribe to shares amounting to $571,428. The
largest bank in Tunisia, Société Tunisienne de
Banque, increased its ownership in SNI and five
local banks bought shares for the first time.[46]

A number of foreign financial institutions participated in the expansion. Among them were Banca
Commerciale Italiana, Bank für Gemeinwirtschaft of
Germany, Caisse Centrale de Cooperation Economique
of France, Caisse des Dépôts et Consignations of

France, and Stockholms Enskilda Bank.   The total resources of SNI after the expansion and reorganization totaled over $11.2 million.[47]

Summary

      IFC's investments in five development finance
companies in five African countries have totaled
slightly over $3.9 million.   IFC has encouraged
several foreign financial institutions to participate in these investments.   Three of these investments helped establish new finance companies.   These
newly formed companies began operations with total
resources of $23.7 million to be used to assist in-
dustrial development in the three countries.   The
SNI reorganization resulted in an institution with
$11.2 million to be used for industrial development.
The IFC-World Bank joint assistance in BNDE in
Morocco added $17 million to the capital resources
of that company.   Thus, well over $50 million in
capital was made available to reinvestment in underdeveloped countries by IFC investment operations in
private development finance companies in Africa.

CHAPTER **8** THE INTERNATIONAL
FINANCE CORPORATION
IN EUROPE

INTRODUCTION

The IFC has made relatively fewer investment
commitments in Europe than it has in other geographical regions. This is principally because
there are few underdeveloped areas in Europe.

The first IFC commitment in Europe was made
in 1960. Half of the sixteen IFC investments in
Europe have been made, however, during the ninth
and tenth fiscal years of IFC operations. These
sixteen investments have been made in five countries to thirteen companies, including nine industrial manufacturing firms and four private development finance companies. IFC has made operational
investments totaling $16,392,439 and one standby
and underwriting commitment of $158,644, for total
investments of $16,551,083. IFC activities are
broken down in Table 14.

These commitments represent less than 10 per
cent of IFC's total activities. However, except
for the Communist-bloc nations and Portugal, these
represent the last of the underdeveloped areas in
Western Europe. In order to better diversify its
commitments geographically, IFC has accelerated investment activities during the last two fiscal
years of the ten-year period. Half of IFC's commitments in Europe were made during those two years
for a total of $8,430,603, or about half the dollar-
volume of total investments by IFC in the area.

Table 14

IFC Investment, Standby and
Underwriting Commitments, 1956-1966,
Europe

Country	Initial Commitment	No. of Commitments	Funds Committed
Finland	1960	4	$ 3,147,645
Greece	1962	5	6,345,002
Italy	1960	1	960,000
Spain	1962	4	3,812,880
Turkey	1963	2	2,285,556
Totals		16	$16,551,083

Source: IFC, Annual Report 1965-1966 (Washington,
          D.C.: International Finance Corporation,
          1966), p. 4.

Table 15 shows the individual investments by
company. Second commitments have been made in
three of the firms and four private development
finance companies are among the recipients of IFC
investment funds.

The purpose of the remainder of this chapter
is to examine closely two IFC commitments in manufacturing firms and IFC activities in four European
private development finance companies. The manufacturing firms are General Cement Company of Greece
and Fábrica Española Magnetos, S.A. (FEMSA) of Spain.
The development finance companies are located in
Finland, Greece, Spain, and Turkey.

GENERAL CEMENT COMPANY, S.A., OF GREECE

Greece is one of the few countries in Western
Europe which is classified as a developing nation.
The country is the southernmost of the Balkan Peninsula and is bordered on the north by Albania, Yugoslavia, and Bulgaria; on the east by the Aegean Sea

Table 15

IFC Commitments in Europe by Company

Company	Country	Operational Investment	Standby and Underwriting
Oy Kutomotuote Ab, Tricol Oy, Toli Oy	Finland	$ 156,000	$ ---
Rauma-Repola Oy	"	1,875,000	---
Teollistamisra-hasto Oy	"	158,644	158,644
Huhtamakiyhtyma Oy	"	799,357	---
Aevol Industrial Company of Organic Fertilizers, S.A.	Greece	600,000	---
"Titan" Cement Company, S.A.	"	1,525,920	---
National Investment Bank for Industrial Development, S.A.	"	719,082	---
General Cement Company, S.A.	"	3,500,000	---
Magrini Meridion-ale, S.p.A.	Italy	960,000	---
Fábrica Española Magnetos, S.A.	Spain	3,227,529	---
Banco del Desarrollo Economico Español, S.A.	"	585,351	---
Turkiye Sinai Kalkinma Bankasi, A.S.	Turkey	916,667	---
Sentetik Iplik Fabrilalari, A.S.	"	1,368,889	---
Totals		$16,392,439	$ 158,644

Source: IFC, Annual Report 1965-1966 (Washington,
          D.C.:   International Finance Corporation,
          1966), Appendix C, pp. 34 and 38.

and Turkey; on the south by the Mediterranean Sea;
and on the west by the Ionian Sea. Greece has
about 8,540,000 inhabitants residing in an area of
50,944 square miles. The capital city is Athens.[1]

The economy's principal enterprise is agriculture with that sector contributing 25 per cent of
Greece's national income in 1965. Forestry and
mining are also important. Industry accounted for
29 per cent of national income in 1965. Greece's
principal exports are tobacco, cotton, fruits, nuts,
olives and olive oil, wine, and sponges in the agricultural sector and iron ore, pyrites, chromite,
and bauxite in the mining sector. The country remains relatively underdeveloped and has a relatively
low per capita national income. Greece has been
admitted to the European Economic Community as an
associate member with a twelve-year adjustment period before becoming a full-fledged member.

The industrialization and growth of the Greek
economy has created a rising demand for cement.
The few large cement producers have been hard-
pressed to keep up with the demand and in recent
years have had to resort to modernization and expansion programs. In two cases, "Titan" Cement
Company and General Cement Company, IFC has participated in expansion programs. One of those commitments, General Cement Company, will be analyzed
in this section.

"Titan" and General are the two largest cement
producers in Greece. Both are relatively the same
size. In 1966, total deliveries by Greek cement
producers amounted to about 3,589,715 tons. Of
this amount, "Titan" delivered 40.21 per cent and
General delivered 39.64 per cent.[2] Thus, about 80
per cent of Greek cement is produced by these two
companies.

Although "Titan" is slightly larger than General and IFC has made commitments in both companies,
General Cement Company was chosen for analysis in
this study. The IFC commitment in General was con-
siderably more than the "Titan" investment and was

much larger than IFC's average commitment. The nature of the investment was also a factor in selecting the General Cement Company as a case study.
IFC did not take an equity interest in General
whereas it did in the "Titan" case. In fact, IFC
seldom commits loan funds without taking some kind
of an equity situation in a project. It is doubted
that IFC will make this kind of investment in the
future.

During early 1966, IFC, along with the National Investment Bank for Industrial Development, S.A.
(NIBID), participated in an expansion program totaling $11.7 million planned by General Cement Com-
pany. General, one of the two largest Greek cement
producers, is owned by more than 500 shareholders.
The shares are traded on the Athens Stock Exchange.
Major interests in the company are owned by a
leading Greek industrial enterprise, the Tsatsos
Group, and by the National Bank of Greece.[3] This
bank is the largest privately owned bank in Greece.

The project application stated that General
had planned an increase in the annual capacity of
its two existing factories from 1.5 million metric
tons to 2.1 million metric tons. In addition, General outlined a proposal for improving the company's
technical efficiency and marketing operations.

The increase in capacity was to be the result
of a new cement unit installed at the company's
Volos facility located in central Greece. The
capacity of this addition was programmed to be
500,000 metric tons per year. Also, a new cement
mill was planned for the Piraeus plant, near Athens.

The marketing operations were to be strengthened by the planned establishment of four new distribution centers, located regionally in Greece and
all having access to water transportation. Such a
center had been opened in 1964 in Salonika.[4]

The IFC investment commitment was a twelve-
year loan of $3.5 million, guaranteed by the Nation-
al Bank of Greece.[5] NIBID joined with IFC in the

project by subscribing to $2 million of debentures
issued by General Cement Company. IFC and NIBID
had previously jointly assisted in financing an expansion of "Titan" Cement Company, S.A., the other
leading Greek cement manufacturer. In 1965, IFC
subscribed to shares in NIBID.

The remaining portion of the financing, approximately $6.2 million, was contributed by existing
shareowners, French and German equipment suppliers,
and the U.S. Export-Import Bank. The latter institution loaned General $2.5 million. A new share
issue resulted in subscriptions for nearly $1.8 mil-
lion and the remainder came from suppliers' credits
offered by the French and German companies.[6]

In accordance with stated objectives, IFC encouraged the participation in a portion of its loan
to General by six American and foreign financial
institutions. The participation amounted to
$975,000. The institutions were: Detroit Bank and
Trust, First National Bank of Chicago, Continental
Illinois National Bank and Trust Company of Chicago,
Svenska Handelsbanken, Kuwait Investment Company,
and Société Financière de Transports et d'Entre-
prises Industrielles (SOFINA) of Brussels.[7]

The project was completed during 1966 and
General was able to achieve greater delivery capacity with the addition of the distribution centers.
This decentralized organization of facilities enabled General to increase its deliveries of bulk
cement. Bulk cement deliveries may constitute 40
per cent or more of total deliveries in most developed countries but they represent a small proportion of Greek cement deliveries.[8] The increase in
General's total deliveries in 1966 was 6 per cent
over those of 1965.[9]

The advantage accruing to the Greek economy
from the expansion program lies in the additional
supply of cement. Cement is the principal construction material in Greece and the increasing construction activity has greatly increased demand for
cement. In the fifteen years since 1950, average

annual use of cement has risen at a rate of 15 per cent. General Cement Company has had to expand and modernize its plant and equipment during this period and the company's production capacity rose nine-fold. This expansion helped the construction industry in Greece, utilized local raw materials, and conserved needed foreign exchange reserves by reducing import demands for cement which would have arisen without the expansion.

At the time of this writing, the political situation in Greece seemed to be in turmoil. During 1967, political events there led to a decline in confidence in the private economic sector. Both private and public construction which had been fore-cast for the latter 1960's were affected adversely. The IFC commitments in both General and "Titan" took into consideration the long-term construction requirements of the Greek economy. This forecast has been affected in the short-run and both com-panies will probably have declining sales and/or excess capacity for the next few years. However, the Greek cement industry has been able to satisfy local demand almost entirely for several years and, when confidence is restored in the Greek economy, these companies will stand to benefit from the backlog of construction needs.

Finally, another unusual factor in the IFC commitments to assist the expansion of the Greek cement industry is that the willingness of IFC to invest in competitive companies is demonstrated. The reasoning underlying such an investment practice is that the competition emanating from these two giants in the Greek cement industry will result in lower costs of production, better distribution pol-icies, increased sales, and greater benefit to the entire Greek economy.[10]

FÁBRICA ESPAÑOLA MAGNETOS, S.A.
(FEMSA) OF SPAIN

Spain, situated on the Iberian peninsula of
Western Europe, has an area of nearly 195,000 square
miles and a population of 31,871,000[11] The country
has generally been a monarchy but since the Spanish
Revolution of the late 1930's, the government has
been dominated by General Francisco Franco who has
held the position of Chief of State of Spain.
Spain is a developing economy which has experienced
a rapid rate of industrialization since 1964.   Much
of the prosperity has been the result of American
foreign aid and a healthy tourist sector.   However,
inflation, neglect of the agriculture sector, and
resulting foreign trade deficits have accompanied
the economic growth.   The principal industries in
Spain are cement, chemicals, food processing, iron
and steel, shipbuilding, and textiles.   The automobile industry has been encouraged by the investment
by Fiat of Italy in SEAT Company of Spain.   Transportation facilities are generally inadequate with
only 60 per cent of the nation's 82,000 miles of
highways being paved, and a rail system, principally
government-owned, consisting of 11,395 miles.[12]
While the rest of Europe is slowing down economically, Spain has experienced a real annual growth
rate in gross national product of 9 per cent with
only a 1 per cent annual growth in population under
the first four-year economic plan.   A new plan
places emphasis on the agricultural sector.   Spain
is also planning to improve political relations
with the rest of Western Europe.   Spain is neither
a member of the European Economic Community nor of
the European Free Trade Association.

The World Bank Group has made other investments
in Spain besides the IFC commitment.   Three World
Bank loans totaling $138 million have been made in
Spanish social overhead capital projects.   No International Development Association credits have been
made to Spain.[13]

IFC made investment commitments in only two
companies in Spain during the 1956-1966 decade.
These were Fábrica Española Magnetos, S.A. (FEMSA),
a manufacturer of automotive electrical equipment,
and Banco del Desarrollo Economico Español, S.A., a
private development finance company. The FEMSA
commitment will be discussed and analyzed in this
section.

FEMSA, a closely held family firm at the time
of IFC's first commitment, was formed in 1940. The
period from 1940 to 1944 was one primarily of preliminary construction. During 1945, FEMSA began
production of electrical equipment for agricultural
machines, electrical systems for vehicles, pumping
systems, and miscellaneous other electrical equipment. Motorcycle electrical equipment production
was begun in 1948 and the growth in this sector was
spectacular in 1953. It was during this period
that the motor vehicle industry in Spain and Europe
began to incur rapid growth.[14]

Achieving rapid growth in the late 1950's and
early 1960's, the company had as many as 1,800 employees by 1962. The company manufactured under
licensing agreements at that time and among its
products were electrical assemblies such as motors
and generators for cars, trucks, tractors, motor-
cycles, and aviation engines. Because of increasing
demand for motor vehicles and engines in Spain,
FEMSA planned an expansion of facilities in 1962.
The owners also wanted to broaden the ownership of
the company. Past expansions had been financed
internally but the company had insufficient capital
and a new public issue of shares was not marketable
at that time. Adequate long-term debt capital
could not be borrowed..

The project proposal was submitted to IFC and
after investigation and analysis of the project,
IFC agreed to commit $3 million of equity and loan
capital. A loan of $2.5 million was made, to be
repaid during the period 1964-1971. In addition,
IFC purchased 30 million pesetas (about $500,000)
in common shares of FEMSA. These shares amounted

to about 13 per cent of the company's issued shares.[15]
The purchase of shares was the first by IFC since
the amendment of IFC's charter in 1961 allowing the
institution to enter into capital share investments.
The FEMSA commitment was also IFC's first financing
arrangement in Spain.

The financing enabled FEMSA to expand its
plant in Madrid, to construct a new factory near
Treto in Santander, and to expand its commercial
and technical assistance facilities in Barcelona.
The share issue was the first step toward broadening the ownership of FEMSA.[16]

IFC, in the performance of its objectives,
encouraged the participation of other private financial institutions and foreign investors in this
investment. Bankers International Financing Company, Inc., of New York, purchased 10 per cent of
IFC's loan and 10 per cent of the shares held by
IFC, for a total participation of $300,000. Dresd-
ner Bank, the second largest German commercial
bank, purchased a portion of IFC's loan totaling
$148,500 of the first maturity.[17]

Further increases in demand for the company's
products led to a firm decision to further expand
the company's productive facilities. The first
IFC-financed expansion by FEMSA had doubled capacity. The expansion had been completed on time
and its total cost was $3.7 million. The new ex-
pansion, planned to begin in 1964, required investment in FEMSA's Madrid and Treto factories and
in its commercial and technical assistance offices
in Valladolid and Vitoria.[18]

In order to facilitate the expansion and plant
improvements, FEMSA increased its share capital
from 230 million pesetas to 345 million pesetas.
In addition, a long-term line of credit was arranged
with Bankers International Financing Company, Inc.,
a subsidiary of Bankers Trust Company of New York.
Bankers International had participated in the first
IFC investment in FEMSA in 1962.[19]

Rights to subscribe to the new issue were established on the basis of one new share of 1,000 pesetas par value for each 2,000 pesetas par value of FEMSA's stock owned by the subscriber. IFC subscribed to 13.5 million pesetas (equivalent to $225,444) of the new issue.[20]

Since the second IFC commitment in FEMSA, eight financial institutions located in Europe, the Middle East, and the United States, have participated in the IFC investments. Of the $2.5 million loan by IFC to FEMSA, all but $1,062,000 had been sold to other investors by 1966 and nearly $275,000 of the equities held by IFC in the company had been sold.[21]

Because of further growth in the automobile and automotive replacement parts industries in Spain, FEMSA was planning another expansion in its plant and equipment in which IFC planned to participate. FEMSA had acquired Autoelectricidad Company of Spain, a manufacturer of products similar to those produced by FEMSA, and this acquisition made FEMSA the third most important producer of automotive electrical equipment in Europe. The company had 4,000 employees by 1966.[22]

The cost of the planned expansion is estimated to be $10.8 million with $2.17 million to come from a new share offering. FEMSA plans to have its shares listed on the Madrid Stock Exchange as a means of broadening the ownership of the company.

The production of FEMSA in standard units increased from 1960 to 1966 by 911 per cent. The company plans to increase its production so that the annual rate of increase from 1960 to 1971 will be 18.4 per cent. Assets of the company have increased from 507.1 million pesetas in 1961 to 1,666.0 million pesetas in 1965. FEMSA's net profit, which includes amortization, increased from 31.1 million pesetas in 1961 to 165 million pesetas in 1966, or a total increase of over 400 per cent.[23]

IFC has been an important factor in encouraging foreign private investment, broadening of ownership,

and expansion of the plant and equipment of a company which was unable in 1962 to acquire adequate
expansion financing from any other source. The
IFC investments have resulted in a company which is
one of the largest manufacturers in one of the most
important industries of Europe. Without this participation, it is doubtful that this could have
happened.

IFC INVESTMENTS IN PRIVATE DEVELOPMENT
FINANCE COMPANIES IN EUROPE

IFC made five investment commitments in four
private development finance companies in four
different European countries during the first decade of its operations. The first two of these
were announced during September, 1963, when IFC
made investments in Teollistamisrahasto Oy (Industrialization Fund) of Finland and the Industrial
Development Bank of Turkey. Three subsequent investments were made in Banco del Desarrollo Economico Español, S.A., of Spain in 1963 and in 1964,
and in the National Investment Bank for Industrial
Development, S.A., of Greece in October, 1965.
These commitments have all been to subscribe to
new shares in the four companies. IFC committed
$2,379,744 in operational investments and another
$158,644 in standby and underwriting commitments,
for total commitments of $2,538,388. The four in-
vestments will be discussed in the following section.

Teollistamisrahasto Oy
(Industrialization Fund) of Finland

The Industrialization Fund of Finland (IFF)
was established in 1954 to assist in the financing
of small- and medium-sized firms in Finland. The
institution was founded with capital amounting to
500,000 Finnish markkas ($158,644). By 1962, the
Fund had total resources of 12 million Finnish
markkas (approximately $3.8 million) from borrowing
and operations. Among its major shareholders were
the three leading Finnish commercial banks,

as well as the Central Bank of Savings Banks,
the Central Bank of Cooperative Societies, and the
Post Office Savings Bank.

Because of the shortage of capital for industrial investment in Finland, smaller firms have had
difficulty financing needed expansion of operations.
Larger companies have been able to obtain local
credit or have acquired funds from foreign investors
Thus, local bankers and the directors of the IFF
decided to expand the resources of the Fund. In
1963, the Bank of Finland, European and American
financial institutions, and local Finnish investors
joined with IFC and the World Bank in furnishing an
additional 50 million Finnish markkas (about $15.6
million) in a financial reorganization of the Fund.[24]

New share capital amounting to slightly over
$4.5 million was issued in the form of Class A and
B shares. Both classes had the same par value but
Class B shares had only one tenth the voting power
of the Class A shares. Finnish shareholders and
European and American financial institutions sub-
scribed to 5 million Finnish markkas ($1.56 million)
in Class A shares. IFC subscribed to 1 million
Finnish markkas ($317,288) of Class A shares but
sold nearly half of this commitment to European and
American financial institutions. Among these were
Brinckmann, Wirtz & Company of Hamburg, Germany;
Chemical International Finance, Ltd., of New York;
Credit Lyonnais S.A.; Deutsche Bank A.G.; Hambros
Bank of London, Ltd.; Northwest International Bank; a
Worms and Cie. IFC retained $159,300 of the share
investment after these participations. In addition
to the Class A shares, the Bank of Finland purchased
all of the Class B shares for $2.8 million.[25]

Besides the equity commitments, the World Bank
loaned IFF approximately $7 million, and shareowners
including the Bank of Finland and the Post Office
Savings Bank, made a loan to the Fund equivalent to
approximately $4.2 million.

Thus, the IFC and World Bank participation in
the Finnish Industrialization Fund assisted the ex-

pansion of the institution's capital resources from
12 million Finnish markkas to 62 million Finnish
markkas, or $19.3 million, an increase of more than
five-fold. The result was an institution better
able to cope with demand for investment funds by
small- and medium-sized industrial firms.

IFF has assisted in the diversification of the
Finnish industrial base by investing in newer industries such as metals, furniture manufacturing, and
textiles. Thus, the country's dependence on timber
and paper has been alleviated.[26] IFF has also made
studies of the Finnish capital market in order to
make recommendations for improving it.[27]

Industrial Development Bank
of Turkey (IDB)

IDB was founded in 1950 and has among its
owners the largest Turkish commercial bank, Turkiye
Is Bankasi, A.S., and nearly 300 other shareholders.
IDB is the principal institution in Turkey for private long-term industrial financing. Chief among
the many industries financed by IDB are food products; stone, earthenware, and glass; textiles; and
metal ore smelting.[28] At the end of 1963, IDB's
total commitments to industrial firms in Turkey exceeded $25 million in loans, credits, and equity
subscriptions.

The World Bank Group had invested in IDB previous to 1963 by making loans in 1950 and 1953,
both amounting to $9 million. The International
Development Association extended a $5 million cre-
dit in 1962 to the Turkish government which in turn
reloaned the credit to IDB.[29] At the time of the
1953 World Bank loan, the capital stock of IDB was
increased.

In September, 1963, a further increase in the
stock of IDB was announced. This was the first
such increase in ten years and amounted to 12.5
million Turkish Lire (LT) of common shares. IFC
participated in this expansion of capital by sub-

scribing to 60 per cent of a new issue sold at 110
per cent of par value. Thus, IFC's investment
amounted to LT 8.25 million, or the equivalent of
$916,667. The remaining 40 per cent was subscribed
by existing shareholders. In addition to this
issue, IDB distributed a stock dividend of LT 12.5
million to the shareowners. After the capital increase, IDB's total capital amounted to LT 50 million, or $5.6 million. IFC's investment in IDB's
stock issued and outstanding was increased to 15
per cent by the operation.

This investment operation by IFC resulted in
increasing the capacity of a private development
finance company which had had a relatively successful history of financing industrial enterprise in a
developing economy. When IDB began its operations,
very few investors bought IDB shares. However, as
a result of seventeen years' successful operations,
IFC participation, and sound IDB marketing programs,
there are over 250 shareowners and IDB's stock is
among the most active on the Istanbul Stock Exchange
IDB had sold over $2 million in shares to over 200
investors by the end of 1965 and, in 1966, was able
to sell another $3 million in shares.[30] The capital
increase by IDB also will permit the institution to
seek debt funds in the future by expanding its
collateral.

In addition to these funds, IDB is able to
borrow many times its own net worth. In 1965, IDB's
net worth amounted to LT 76 million. In 1966, the
Turkish government turned over LT 382 million of
agency funds which IDB had been managing to IDB in
the form of a long-term loan subordinated to all
other IDB debt and capital shares. IDB had been
limiting its borrowing to four times its net worth.
Because the government, as junior creditor, assumes
the risk of the subordinated loan, IDB could include
the loan in its borrowing base and, utilizing the
4:1 ratio, could borrow an amount up to 24 times
the company's net worth.[31]

Banco del Desarrollo Economico Español,
S.A. (BANDESCO) of Spain

During the early 1960's, a World Bank mission
was requested by the Spanish government to make an
economic survey of the country. As a result of
this study, the government initiated the First Economic Plan of 1964-1967. In addition to the ini-
tiation of public economic planning in Spain, the
World Bank Mission recommended broadening the Spanish capital market and improving the channels for
medium- and long-term capital to industrial firms.

A new private development finance company was
established for the purpose of implementing the
World Bank Mission's recommendations about the
Spanish capital market. The Banco del Desarrollo
Economico Español, S.A. (BANDESCO) was the result
of a joint investment venture including IFC, Spain's
leading commercial bank: Banco Español de Credito,
and French, German, Italian, British, and American
private financial institutions.

The new financing institution was established
to underwrite and distribute shares of industrial
enterprises in Spain and to encourage other local
financial institutions to participate in these investments. In addition, BANDESCO would offer technical advice concerning financial and managerial
problems. Besides the Banco Español de Credito,
another leading Spanish bank, Banco Guipuzcoano,
also became a shareowner.

IFC committed $291,667 in BANDESCO by pur-
chasing 17.5 million pesetas of shares. IFC encouraged several foreign financial institutions to
participate in the project. Among these were Banca
Commerciale Italiana, Barclays Bank D.C.O., Deutsche
Bank A.G., Morgan Guaranty International Finance
Corporation, and de Rothschild Frères of France.[32]

BANDESCO incurred rapid growth after its in-
ception in 1963. From late 1963 until April 30,
1965, BANDESCO approved project proposals amounting

to $39.5 million in over 100 enterprises located in
Spain. During this time, the company made three
bond issues totaling $25 million. BANDESCO utilizes
public bond issues as its major source of revenue.[33]
BANDESCO is one of the few development finance companies in which IFC has invested which acquires its
capital principally from the private sector through
these debenture issues These debentures are
backed by the credit evolving from BANDESCO's close
cooperations with Banco Español de Credito. Thus,
by late 1964, directors of BANDESCO decided to increase common shares outstanding in order to expand
the company's borrowing ability.[34]

Therefore, BANDESCO made a new share offering
in 1964 amounting to 210 million pesetas, or about
$3.5 million. IFC subscribed to 17.5 million pese-
tas, or $291,911, the same amount of shares as IFC's
first participation in 1963.[35] All of the original
shareholders, previously named, exercised their
rights in the new issue.

The BANDESCO commitment by IFC established an
institution which has facilitated improved financing
of industrial enterprise in Spain. The institution
has significant Spanish sponsorship and several foreign financial institutions have been encouraged to
participate in the project, thus making more international the interest in a developing economy. The
magnitude of BANDESCO's investments during the first
two years of operations lends credence to the implication that an institution such as BANDESCO was
needed in Spain.

National Investment Bank for Industrial
Development, S.A. (NIBID) of Greece

NIBID had been established by the Bank of
Greece and leading American and European financial
institutions as a private development finance company with the purposes of furnishing Greek enterprises with medium- and long-term financing, assisting in developing a Greek capital market, and facilitating joint ventures between Greek and foreign
investors.

In October, 1965, NIBID announced a new share
offering to increase the capital base of the company so that NIBID would be able to satisfy increased demand for investment capital by the growing
Greek economy. The company's shares were increased
from 180 million drachmas to 300 million drachmas
($6 million to $10 million). IFC subscribed to
shares equivalent to $719,082. This investment
made IFC's holdings equal to those of NIBID's
largest shareowner.[36]

A number of leading American and European financial institutions are among NIBID's shareholders.
They are: Chase International Investment Corporation, Deutsche Bank A.G., Banca di Credito Finan-
ziario S.p.A., Hambros Bank of London, Ltd., Manufacturers Hanover International Banking Corporation,
Banque Lambert, Compagnie Financière et Industrielle S.A., Svenska Handelsbanken, Banque
Nationale pour le Commerce et l'Industrie S.A.,
Credit Lyonnais, Credit Commercial de France S.A.,
Credit Suisse, and Nordfinanz-Bank.[37]

NIBID is more liberal than most private development finance companies in its operating policy in
that it will invest an amount up to 20 per cent of
its share capital and surplus in an equity commitment and up to 25 per cent in a single investment.
Few such companies will exceed 15 per cent. In
addition, NIBID devotes about half its investments
to new enterprises.[38]

Summary

IFC's investments in these four private development finance companies have amounted to $2,538,388.
In three of the cases, the investments were participations in expansions of existing institutions. In
the other, IFC helped establish BANDESCO in Spain
and also participated in a subsequent expansion of
the capital of that company.

Furthermore, these companies financed by IFC
have channeled investment funds in newly formed or

expanding industrial enterprises in large amounts,
and their capital resources are relatively large
for their roles.   In addition, these finance companies have encouraged many foreign financial institutions to enter joint ventures in local projects
and have assisted in rendering financial and managerial advisory services to local industrial firms.

9

THE INTERNATIONAL FINANCE CORPORATION AND ITS OPERATIONAL PROBLEMS

INTRODUCTION

Because of the nature of its operations, the International Finance Corporation incurs many problems. Most or all of these troublesome areas can be overcome in the long run but, as with any private enterprise venture, IFC operates in the relatively short run. These obstacles are incurred at different levels of IFC operations and in various time spans.

Four problem areas are significant in the activities of IFC. First, there are the short-comings which are found and inherent in the less developed countries (LDC's) themselves. Second, companies in which IFC has invested have some serious problems to overcome because of the economic systems found in LDC's. Third, IFC incurs specific problems in its day-to-day operations which affect its role in development finance. Fourth, general problem areas exist in IFC's work which offer great challenges in the fulfilling of its goals. The future of the International Finance Corporation presents many questions whose answers may supply the necessary ingredients in winning the world's war on poverty and underdevelopment. These problem areas will be analyzed in the following sections.

PROBLEMS INHERENT IN THE NATURE OF LDC'S

A number of difficulties exist in LDC's which are derived from the conditions inherent in under-developed economies. The degree and number of these problems depend upon the relative position of the economy and political structure of an LDC when compared with those of all other LDC's. The urgent needs of these countries in alleviating the poverty, disease, and illiteracy will be satisfied only when these inherent, and sometimes latent, problems are alleviated or eliminated. The growth of the private sector and the speed of this growth may be determined, in great measure, by the success in any attempts to reduce these problems.

The Cultural Problem

Various operational problems are present in every LDC and these complicate doing business. They take the form of varying customs, languages, laws, and conditions which are prevalent from one LDC to another.[1] These cultural differences are among the most significant hindrances to world trade and development and an understanding of their source may be the key to the successful practice of private enterprise in the LDC's. Maneck S. Wadia speaks of a "concept of culture" and relates it to marketing. He states that the impact of this concept on marketing is endless.[2] Edward Hall discusses the "silent language" when he analyzes the cultural differences in LDC's in regard to the amount of space which should separate people in conversation, the different emphasis placed on the commodity of time by foreigners in many LDC's, as well as other "silent" elements of subtle cultural differences.[3] James Lee analyzes a person's self-reference criterion as "the unconscious reference to one's own cultural values" and further states that this is a most serious stumbling-block in international business.[4] It is the cultural analysis of these problems which is one prerequisite to successful private enterprise ventures in the LDC's. And it is

this area of cultural differences among LDC's which
complicates the process of applying IFC's standards
and criteria uniformly, fairly, and successfully.[5]

LDC Governmental Restrictions and Policies

It follows, therefore, that a great deal of
misunderstanding and miscommunication between LDC's
and the industrialized nations has resulted from
these cultural differences. Thus, many restrictions
have been placed by governments of LDC's on private
foreign investment. Such restrictions have placed
a damper on the flows of private foreign funds into
the LDC's and the result has been slower growth in
these countries than might have been possible in
the absence of such restrictions.

Governmental consultants and aid missions from
the industrialized nations report that many of
these obstacles exist although the situation is
being improved constantly. Among the problems
which inhibit private foreign investment are nationalistic arguments against such investment, unfair
and unnecessary limitations on the amount of control
of local business firms by foreign investors, and
restrictions which unnecessarily inhibit employment
of foreign managerial and technical personnel.[6]
Some LDC's limit the amount of foreign ownership in
a local firm to a minority interest and some re-
strict ownership to fifty-fifty joint ventures.
Many foreign companies will not consider investments,
especially in LDC's, in which a majority interest
is precluded.

Because of the nationalistic practices of some
LDC's, economic policies are formulated which are
unsound and which lead to further problems. Governmental financial policies often result in inflation and, occasionally, devaluation of a nation's
currency. An LDC may impose an inordinate tax rate
on the profits of local firms owned by foreign interests. Governmental red tape and inefficient
bureaucracy are prevalent in the LDC's and dis-
courage private foreign investment. The fear of

nationalization or expropriation of foreign plant
and equipment is highly justified in many developing
countries. Foreign investors find it very difficult to be altruistic in searching for new investment projects and the goals of profit maximization
and risk minimization actually become two of the
most significant problems in the attempts of the
LDC's to industrialize with the assistance of private foreign investment.

Inadequate Personnel

Finally, an inherent problem very prevalent in
the LDC's is the lack of trained and experienced
personnel. Technological, managerial, and entrepreneurial personnel are in short supply in the
developing economies. A great deal is said about
the so-called technological gap. This generally
refers to the transfer of technical personnel from
Europe to the United States but somewhat the same
phenomenon is occurring from the LDC's to the industrialized nations, thus widening the gap between
the two groups of nations.

Without an adequate supply of trained people
and without the competition which results from
entrepreneurial activity, cottage industry and
monopoly interests will remain prevalent in the
LDC's. Thus, inefficiency and economic exploita-
tion will continue to be a way of life.

Some LDC's are making strong advances in training and education. Some are including human resources as one of the prime elements in their economic plans. The Republic of Korea is one of these
nations and it became one of the few governments to
publish a plan on science and technology. This
plan is supplementary to its Second Five-year Economic Development Plan, 1967-1971.[7]

PROBLEMS OF PRIVATE ENTERPRISE IN LDC'S

Close Family Ownership

Several impediments to effective and economical business operations in LDC's exist within private enterprise and the micro-operations of the
companies themselves. One of these problems is the
traditional practice of close family control or
ownership of many enterprises in LDC's. Thus, outside ownership and the increased capital it brings
with it is inhibited because the family is reluctant
to share in the ownership of the firm. The family-
owned firm may be opposed to local as well as foreign ownership.[8]

Such traditional practice of ownership has
certain adverse side-effects. Modern companies,
especially in the more important manufacturing industries, require broader ownership. Broader ownership brings with it more and better ideas. The
managerial techniques necessary for today's more
complex operations may be more easily obtainable.
The lack of executive management personnel is a
prevalent problem in the LDC's and close family
ownership may perpetuate this as well as obsolete
and inefficient operating techniques and practices.
In addition, this practice represses research and
development funds which outside equity capital
could furnish and which are necessary for dynamic
growth of private enterprise in LDC's.

Family-controlled enterprise generally develops
primarily from retained earnings. These funds are
usually inadequate to finance the expansion of many
firms such as those producing steel, paper, and
cement, whose markets are rapidly expanding in the
LDC's.

Problems Created by Lack of
Experienced Personnel

The lack of experienced administrative personnel causes specific difficulties to arise. Inadequate financial management is practiced. Reporting
of operations is relatively poor and planning and
organizing based on this reporting results in inefficient operations. Many of these firms require
outside technological advice in order to survive.
In most cases, this advice comes only with outside
ownership.

A number of companies in which IFC has committed
investment funds have found that outside ownership
and its subsequent technological and managerial expertise resulted in expanded operations and greater
profits. Japanese interests overcame many local
problems in the Arewa Textiles Company project in
Nigeria.[9] The technological and managerial advice
offered by the Japanese resulted in one of the minor
miracles of African development. In the cases of
NPK-Engrais, S.A.T. in Tunisia[10] and Packages, Ltd.
in Pakistan,[11] two companies in which IFC invested,
Swedish interests contributed technological advisory
services and management development programs which
have greatly assisted these two projects.

Reporting Procedures

Accounting procedures in reporting operations
are generally of inferior quality in developing
countries. Accounting standards either do not
exist or are weak in nature. Companies may operate
in the same geographical region but practice entirely different accounting procedures. Such an
example is illustrated by the cases of Ismail
Cement Industries of India and Packages, Ltd. of
Pakistan, described in Chapter 6. Packages pub-
lishes a very elaborate and presentable annual report which compares favorably with reports published
by most leading American companies. On the other
hand, Ismail Cement's annual report uses a format

that is not very informative and, in the case of a
number of items, is ambiguous and confusing.

However, with the assistance and prodding of
IFC, reporting procedures are improving among those
companies which have obtained IFC commitments.
Several IFC officials have suggested that many
problems in reporting have been overcome but,
nevertheless, accounting standards in the LDC's
are still relatively primitive.

Cost Overruns

A further problem may stem from the lack of
adequate and experienced financial management in
the LDC's. Many projects in the developing countries suffer from cost overruns after the project
is begun. These overruns may result from poor financial forecasts or from unforeseen problems.
Overruns may and do occur in the industrialized
nations but, perhaps, with less frequency. IFC reported in 1960 that in the thirty-three commitments
made during IFC's first four years of operations,
about half had incurred overruns ranging from 10 to
50 per cent above original estimates.[12] IFC requires that provision for overruns be made during
the negotiations prior to commitment of its funds
to a project.

Miscellaneous Technical Problems

Finally, a number of miscellaneous technical
problems may arise in company operations in the
LDC's. Such problems as market appraisal, length
of time before production begins, and devaluation
of the local currency are the most important of
these problems.

Market surveys are more difficult to obtain in
LDC's because telephone facilities or postal systems
are poorly developed or because statistics and
other data are inadequate. There is a generally
high level of illiteracy in most LDC's and, thus,

questionnaires are not easily utilized. Door-to-
door surveys may not be practicable because of cultural inhibitions. In addition, the fear of putting
anything in writing is prevalent in the LDC's.[13]

Another technical problem which companies in
LDC's face is the time necessary to move a new project on stream. Construction, financing, and
staffing all require more time than these functions
do in industrialized nations. Material and machinery, as well as personnel, may be scarce. Therefore, planning for such projects must take into
consideration a longer period of time to completion.[1]

Finally, devaluation of local currency may
result in the problem of obtaining financial resources necessary for project implementation.[15]
Governmental policies such as devaluation, whose
timing cannot generally be forecast, have happened
in a number of countries in which are located firms
assisted by IFC in their financing. Among these
countries are Argentina, Finland, and India.

IFC'S PROBLEMS OF DAY-TO-DAY OPERATIONS

The International Finance Corporation faces a
number of problems in its day-to-day operations.
Applying the same standards and criteria from project to project requires a patience and wisdom
which few international organizations find in great
supply. In fact, there is some doubt, after a
lengthy analysis, whether such application is
possible or practicable. However, three principal
problems in this category are worthy of discussion.
One concerns project evaluation and forecasting the
future of certain ventures in certain LDC's. A
second concerns the difficulty of finding appropriate and feasible projects which are profitable.
Finally, the promotion of entrepreneurial capacity
in the LDC's is an extremely bothersome obstacle.

Project Evaluation

Forecasting the future of any new project is risky business. Many unforeseen circumstances may occur. Inexperienced personnel may overlook important information in the project survey. Government policies in the host country may adversely affect a realistic forecast.

IFC has invested in a number of companies which have later been confronted by some of these problems. An inadequate market survey resulted in overestimated forecasts for the production and subsequent profitability of Fertilizantes Sinteticos, S.A., a fertilizer producer located in Peru.[16] The market forecast for the output of Mulco Textiles, Limited, a Ugandan textiles manufacturer, was drastically curtailed by the political breakup of the East African Common Market, a regional bloc of three nations whose combined markets were the foundation of the Mulco forecast.[17] In addition to these cases, financial forecasts have been affected by devaluations of local currency systems in Colombia, Finland, India, as well as other countries.

Inadequacy of Feasible Projects

Another problem IFC faces constantly is the difficulty in finding appropriate projects which satisfy its investment criteria. Local and foreign private enterprise should normally accept the best and most profitable projects; whereas, other less profitable projects may be vitally needed by the local economies.

A good example of this problem is illustrated by analysis of IFC's first two years of operations. Of the 235 project applications submitted to IFC during this period, only 7 per cent proved to be feasible and not all of these were accepted by IFC for commitments.[18] Many reasons are given for the low number of acceptable projects. Nearly half prove to be ineligible under IFC's investment criteria.

One of the principal limitations on agricultural growth in LDC's is the lack of well-planned
investment projects. Many analysts have assumed
that a shortage of capital was the major limitation
facing agriculture in the developing countries.
However, the real problem is poor planning resulting
from the experienced manpower shortage in LDC's.
IFC and the World Bank have cooperated with the
United Nations' Food and Agriculture Organization
to lend technical assistance to the agricultural
sectors of these countries.[19]

Industrial Promotion

Finally, IFC has found that the promotion of
entrepreneurial capacity in the LDC's is one of
its greatest challenges and a principal function
in fulfilling its objectives. The inadequacy of
private entrepreneurs creates the need for some
institutional arrangement for promotion. Although
industrial promotion is costly and requires capa-
bilities not always present in financial institutions, IFC has maintained a successful record of
promoting industrial growth in the LDC's.

IFC has, on occasion, initiated surveys which
have led to a project commitment. It has brought
together local capital and management and foreign
technical expertise in projects such as NPK-Engrais
in Tunisia, Arewa Textiles, Limited, in Nigeria,
PASA in Argentina, Mahindra-Ugine Steel Company in
India, and Packages, Ltd. in Pakistan.

In addition, IFC performs underwriting and
standby activities in new equity issues made by
private companies. One of the most significant
underwriting operations by IFC concerned a leading
Mexican steel manufacturer, Compañia Fundidora de
Fierro y Acero de Monterrey, S.A. (Fundidora). IFC
underwrote Fundidora shares in 1962, 1964, and 1966.
These investments totaled over $16 million and have
been instrumental in assisting Fundidora to greatly
expand its capacity.[20]

Martin Rosen, Executive Vice President of IFC, said the following about industrial promotion in a speech in Caracas, Venezuela, in 1964:

> By proper promotional activity, an individual financing institution can help to break down obstacles in the path of industrial progress. The institution's financial resources, its technical staff and its contacts with both domestic and international investors may give it some of the means of doing so. Its ability to originate ventures, to help prepare projects and take the lead in modifying proposals submitted to it, are vital elements in its normal operations.[21]

SOME GENERAL PRESENT-DAY PROBLEMS OF IFC OPERATIONS

A number of general problems have arisen which require answers if IFC is to adequately fulfill the objectives specified in its charter and if it is to retain its role as one of the free world's most important and successful international financial institutions. These problems may be presented in the form of questions. What directions should IFC take in the future if it is to fulfill its charter objectives as well as those of the World Bank Group? This question ties in with a second problem which some analysts have said is a criticism of IFC. Has IFC been too businesslike and conservative in its operations? Perhaps it has not taken a sufficiently high risk although its commitments are made in underdeveloped countries without government guarantee.

Another significant question which might be asked about IFC concerns its financing operations and, therefore, becomes a problem area. What should be the optimum size of IFC's portfolio? How to keep revolving its funds so as not to get in a bind may become a critical question if IFC reaches the point where it has exhausted the present borrowing arrange-

ment it has with the World Bank. Two diverse view-
points seem to exist about the speed of revolving
IFC's portfolio. One viewpoint suggests that the
portfolio be revolved as quickly as possible and
that this will be possible. Another viewpoint is
that some optimum size of the portfolio will be
attained and that turnover of the securities in the
portfolio will then become more and more difficult.
Coupled with a narrowing spread in interest rates
between what IFC will have to pay the World Bank
for borrowed funds and the rates which IFC will be
able to charge its clients in the LDC's, such a
viewpoint suggests less profitable operations in the
future. However, the ability of IFC to borrow from
the World Bank might be more unlimited than the
present borrowing ceiling imposed by the charter
amendment. If IFC's operations became cramped, a
higher debt ceiling could be implemented in the
same manner as was the present four-to-one limitation

    As new directions are taken in IFC's commit-
ments in areas which are relatively new to it, such
as tourism and agribusiness, a new expertise must
be created within the organization. This has not
been a problem in the past but the small size of
IFC's present staff may lead to the necessity for
its drastic expansion. The World Bank will also
increase its demands upon IFC's personnel in industrial projects which it submits to IFC for study
and approval. Thus, a much larger staff or more
utilization of outside consultants may become
necessary.

    Finally, through interviews with IFC officials
and personal observations of their operations, one
trait has been noticed which may create a latent
problem resulting in the unintentional inhibition
of IFC's future growth, especially when a very
dynamic and geometric growth may be necessary.
This is the inability, so it seems, of IFC officials
to see IFC as something much more than just another
case study in the realm of developmental financing
institutions. Although there is agreement among
these personnel that IFC is a unique institution,
few see it as a tremendously exciting organization

which is serving as the catalyst leading to dynamic growth of private enterprise in the LDC's.

There may be two reasons for this. First, the nature of the duties of IFC officials may have caused them to suppress any emotionalism about the institution. However noble this characteristic may be, it may have contributed to the lack of knowledge by the general public, especially in the United States, of IFC's operations. Secondly, IFC personnel are specialists who are highly capable in narrow technological areas. This narrowness of their job descriptions may have limited their outlook and view of the total organization. If the need ever arises whereby IFC will have to do some drastic selling among its members for additional support, such a more romantic outlook may be rewarding.

CONCLUSIONS

A number of problems have been delineated which are inherent in the LDC's, present within the private enterprise sector in these nations, or which face IFC either specifically in its daily operations or generally in its over-all fulfillment of charter objectives and future operations. In time, as development continues and accelerates in the LDC's, those problems created by cultural variations and limited resources will be alleviated or eliminated. As IFC continues to learn from its experiences and to grow in its operations, solutions should be found to its daily operating problems. Only the future holds the answers to the general problems which face the International Finance Corporation.

CHAPTER **10** A DECADE OF
OPERATIONS:
SUMMARY AND
EVALUATION

SUMMARY

One of the objectives of this study is to make
an evaluation of IFC's operations during its first
decade of existence, 1956-1966. A number of case
studies of IFC investments have been presented in
Chapters 5 through 8. These cases were selected to
demonstrate the variety of functions performed by
IFC as well as the variety of companies in which
IFC has invested. In the following sections, the
total activities of IFC's first ten years of operations will be drawn together, summarized, and presented as a whole, and the analysis of this data
will furnish the basis for an evaluation.

The International Finance Corporation was
established for the purpose of assisting the development of lower income countries which are members
of the World Bank by investing in private enterprise projects located in these countries. IFC was
established with the unique characteristic of implementing this objective without government guarantee. The charter of IFC was later amended to
permit a further characteristic unique among international developmental financing institutions: IFC
was permitted to take an equity position in projects
which it accepted.

Membership and Share Capital

During the first decade of IFC's operations, membership and capital have increased significantly. Table 16 shows that membership increased from thirty-one nations to eighty-one and that the increase in share capital during the period was from $78.0 to $99.4 million.

IFC membership has increased significantly in only two fiscal years, according to Table 16. In the first fiscal year 1956-1957, the membership of IFC increased by 58 per cent. This large increase was probably a result of the publicizing of the establishment of IFC and some of these memberships probably represented nations which were unable to be charter members for one reason or another. During the fiscal year 1962-1963 ten new members were added for an increase of 16 per cent. There was little or no increase in membership in all other fiscal years. The 1962-1963 increase included eight African nations, including some newly formed nations. This was a period when IFC began to increase its interest in Africa.

IFC Commitments 1956-1966

Since the first year of IFC operations when four investments totaling $5,320,000 were made in companies located in Brazil, Chile, and Mexico, IFC has averaged over thirteen commitments annually. All told, commitments were made during 1956-1966 amounting to $172,361,343. These were made to 100 companies located in thirty-four countries.[1] Thus, the average size of these commitments is $1.39 million on an individual project basis and $1.72 million on a per company basis.

IFC has made commitments to projects located in all five continental areas outside North America. Its most active area of interest has been in the Western Hemisphere: Central and South America. Approximately 56 per cent of IFC's investments have

Table 16

Membership and Share Capital,
1956—1966

	1956	1957	1958	1959	1960	1961	1962	1963	1964	1965	1966
Membership[a]	31	49	55	57	59	59	63	73	78	78	81
Share Capital ($ millions)	78	92.4[b]	93.3	94	96.5	96.6	96.5	98.2	99	99	99.4

[a]Initial

[b]September 10, 1957

Source: Annual Reports of IFC, 1956-1966.

182

been made in this area and these Latin American
companies have received 58 per cent of funds committed by IFC. Fifteen investments have been made
in Colombian enterprises and twelve commitments
have been made in Mexican companies.

Companies located in Asia and the Middle East
have received the second highest proportion of IFC
investments. Twenty-two investments have been made
in this area. This represents 18 per cent of IFC's
total commitments as well as 18 per cent of total
funds invested. Of these twenty-two commitments,
Indian firms have received nine and Pakistani enterprises have received seven.

European companies have received 13 per cent
of the commitments and slightly less than 10 per
cent of the funds which IFC has invested. Of the
sixteen commitments made in Europe, thirteen have
gone to companies located in Finland, Greece, and
Spain. Few remaining underdeveloped areas exist in
Western Europe.

Africa received fourteen IFC commitments during
the 1956-1966 period. These represented 11 per cent
of total commitments and 13 per cent of funds approved for investment by IFC. Interest in Africa
has been increasing in the last few years. These
investments were well spread in Africa and no member
nation received more than two IFC investments.
Finally, Australia received three commitments totaling $975,000 during the early years of IFC
operations.[2]

During the period 1956-1966, most of IFC's investments were made to companies in the industrial
sector. A breakdown of these investments is presented in Table 17.

The table obviously points out the trend toward heavy emphasis on iron and steel, paper, and
cement manufacturing companies during the first
decade of operations. Over half the funds committed
by IFC were invested in these industries.

Table 17

Industry Breakdown,
IFC Investments 1956-1966

Industry	Amount	Percentage
Iron and Steel	$ 46.8 m.	27.1 %
Pulp and Paper	26.8	15.5
Construction Materials	22.1	12.8
Development Finance Companies	18.9	11.0
Textiles	17.1	9.9
Chemicals	12.0	7.0
Food Processing	10.5	6.1
Other	18.2	10.6
Totals	$172.4 m.	100.0 %

Source: IFC, Annual Report 1965-1966 (Washington,
         D.C.: International Finance Corporation,
         1966), p. 5.

Standby and Underwriting

One of IFC's major functions is its standby
and underwriting activities. As part of the role
it plays in the promotion of private enterprise,
IFC may agree to subscribe to part of a company's
future equity issue or it may underwrite a new
offering in order to encourage other private financial institutions or local investors to participate
in the cost of a project.

IFC made total investments amounting to
$25,054,317 in original standby and underwriting
commitments during the period 1956-1966.[3] These
commitments were made to eleven companies in ten
countries. Of these, five were private development
finance companies. Over 60 per cent of these investments were made to two companies in Mexico. In
fact, nearly 59 per cent was invested in one leading

steel company, Compañia Fundidora de Fierro y Acero
de Monterrey, S.A., in 1962, 1964, and 1966.[4]

IFC encouraged participation by other private
investors, among them many foreign private financial institutions. After participation by sub-
underwriters and acquisition by others, IFC acquired
only $3,595,789 of these standby and underwriting
investments, or roughly one seventh of the total.
The IFC operations in this area are summarized in
Table 18.

Development Finance Companies

Beginning in 1962, IFC became totally respon-
sible for World Bank Group activities in investments in private development finance companies (DFC's).
The evaluation of project investment applications
submitted by existing DFC's and the promotion of
new institutions of this type became two of IFC's
most important operations.

As of June 30, 1966, the World Bank Group had
committed funds totaling $491.8 million to 25 DFC's
in 21 countries. IFC's total investments including
loans, underwriting, and equity subscriptions in 17
DFC's located in 15 countries totaled $18,545,787.
Total disbursements amounted to $14.1 million.[5]
The 25 DFC's which had received World Bank Group
financing had committed investment funds amounting
to approximately $1.5 billion, principally to local
small industrial enterprises whose projects were
too small to be considered by IFC. As of December
31, 1966, these 25 DFC's had capital resources
amounting to slightly more than $1 billion.[6]

Thus, of the financial resources available to
the 25 DFC's, almost half represented World Bank
Group financing. The World Bank Group was able to
accomplish $1.5 billion of development financing
through DFC's with total investment of $492 million.
Thus, other investment funds totaled about $2.05
for every dollar contributed by the World Bank Group.
The ratio of investments made by the 17 DFC's in

Table 18

Standby and Underwriting Commitments, 1956-1966

Country and Company	Original Commitment	Amount Acquired by IFC
COLOMBIA		
Forjas de Colombia, S.A.	$ 352,109	$ 176,548
COSTA RICA		
Productos de Concreto, S.A.	310,810	228,612
ETHIOPIA		
Ethiopian Pulp and Paper, S.A.	1,700,000	---
FINLAND		
Industrialization Fund	158,644	635
LIBERIA		
Liberian Bank for Industrial Development and Investment	250,000	248,950
MALAYSIA		
Malaysian Industrial Development Finance, Ltd.	490,000	---
MEXICO		
Compañia Fundidora de Fierro y Acero de Monterrey, S.A. (1962)	2,944,856	751,853
Compañia Fundidora de Fierro y Acero de Monterrey, S.A. (1964)	6,100,000	1,310

Country and Company	Original Commitment	Amount Acquired by IFC
Compañia Fundidora de Fierro y Acero de Monterrey, S.A. (1966)	$ 5,724,303	$ 2,948
Tubos de Acero de Mexico, S.A.	750,000	150,000
NIGERIA		
Nigerian Industrial Development Bank, Ltd.	1,400,000	1,399,516
PHILIPPINES		
Private Development Corporation of the Philippines	4,359,063	205,217
VENEZUELA		
Dominguez y Cia.- Caracas, S.A.	514,541	430,200
Totals	$25,054,317	$ 3,595,789

Source: IFC, Annual Report 1965-1966 (Washington, D.C.: International Finance Corporation, 1966), p. 41.

which IFC has invested to the amount of IFC's total
investment in the 17 companies, $18.5 million, is
even more dramatic. The portfolios of these 17
companies, measured between January 1, 1965, and
August 31, 1965, approximated between $400-450 mil-
lion depending upon the exchange rates in effect
during that period.[7] Thus, the combined portfolios
of these 17 companies was more than 20 times the
combined IFC investment commitments in these institutions.

In addition to the investment and promotional
activities of IFC in DFC's, it has extended management advisory services to them and has been invited
to serve on the boards of 10 DFC's in which it is a
shareholder.[8] Also, IFC has joined with some of
these DFC's in investing funds in 16 companies in 9
countries, principally in cases where a project's
requirements could not be met by a local capital
market or a local DFC.

Joint Ventures

IFC has been quite successful in its industrial promotional role of bringing together the
optimum partnership in many of the projects it has
financed. IFC has done this by combining local
ownership with its knowledge of the market and its
ability to obtain labor and maintain good relations
with the government, with foreign ownership interests which have been able to inject technical,
managerial, and administrative skills into the
enterprise.

Several joint venture arrangements are among
the 100 companies financed by IFC. Some examples
in which the foreign partner has contributed expertise that has greatly assisted project implementation are: 1) Packages, Ltd., a packaging materials
producer, with local Pakistani interests combined
with Swedish investment; 2) NPK-Engrais, S.A.T., a
fertilizer producer, with Swedish and local Tunisian investors; 3) Mahindra-Ugine Steel Company, a
steel producer, with French and local Indian

interests combined; and 4)Arewa Textiles Limited, a
Nigerian textiles manufacturer, with local Nigerian
interests combined with a Japanese syndicate's investment.

FINANCIAL RECORD

Total Commitments

A financial analysis of IFC's operations
during 1956-1966 will be presented in this section.
The amount of yearly gross commitments, as well as
cumulative totals, made by IFC as of the end of
each fiscal year, is shown in Table 19.

Table 19

Gross Commitments
($ millions where funds are noted)

Year	Number of Commitments	Funds Committed	Average Size of Commitments	Cumulative Total
1957	4	$ 4.3	$ 1.1	$ 4.3
1958	7	6.1	0.9	10.4
1959	13	10.4	0.8	20.8
1960	13	21.8	1.7	42.6
1961	9	6.2	0.7	48.8
1962	9	21.3	2.4	70.1
1963	11	18.0	1.6	88.1
1964	18	20.8	1.2	108.9
1965	15	26.0	1.7	134.9
1966	21	35.6	1.7	170.5*

*adjusted to $172.4 million because of ex-
change rate adjustments and rounding errors.

Source: IFC Annual Reports, 1956-1966.

From this table, a number of operational factors are found to be significant. During the first
three years of activity, average investments by IFC
were quite small, averaging less than $1 million
each. A backlog of projects probably caused the
large commitment of funds in fiscal year 1960,
actually doubling the cumulative total of the first
three years. The highest commitment average occurred in 1962. This was the year IFC was allowed by
charter amendment to invest directly in the equities
of its clients. In addition, a Development Bank
Services Department was established and the first
major commitments by IFC in DFC's were made in
Colombia. Nearly half of all IFC commitments were
made during the last four years of the decade and
40 per cent were placed in fiscal years 1964, 1965,
and 1966, when cumulative total investments nearly
doubled.

Equity Investment

Since the change allowing equity participation,
IFC has invested in the equities of 52 companies
located in 27 countries, as of June 30, 1966.[9] Its
portfolio at that time amounted to $84 million, of
which $28.9 million, or 34.4 per cent, represented
shareownership. This ability to subscribe to shares
enabled IFC to participate in the ownership of some
17 DFC's located 15 countries and to underwrite the
shares of industrial companies.

Total Disbursements

Although IFC has made investment commitments
totaling $172.4 million, its disbursements during
1956-1966 were much less than this amount, principally because of cancellations, terminations, repayments, and participations by other investors.
IFC's cumulative commitments, net of cancellations
and terminations, were $161.2 million and the cumu-
lative total of disbursements was $114.6 million.
These data are presented in Table 20.

Table 20

Various IFC Financial Data
($ millions)

Item	Cumulative 1956-1966	
Capital	99.4	
Net Income	26.4	
Net Profit on Sales of Investments	2.4	
Net Other Losses	(0.5)	
Repayments of Investments	12.4	
Sales of Investments	34.8	
Acquisitions by Others of Secur- ities covered by Standby and Underwriting Commitments	18.0	
Total of Funds Available		192.9
Gross Commitments Made	172.4	
Less Cancellations and Terminations	11.2	
Less Exchange Adjustments	.6	
Net Commitments Made		160.6
Uncommitted Funds at June 30, 1966		32.3

Source: IFC, Annual Report 1965-1966 (Washington,
          D.C.:   International Finance Corporation,
          1966), p. 17.

A number of activities are noticeable from
data in Table 20. One principal source of funds
for IFC operations is the sale of investments from
its portfolio. A total of $34.8 million of invest-
ments have been sold representing commitments in
fifty companies located in twenty-six countries.
Approximately half of these investments were located
in Brazil, Colombia, Mexico, and Peru, and were,
thus, among the most seasoned of IFC's investments.

Although there has been some defaulting in interest and/or principal payments by some firms whose securities are contained in its present portfolio, only two losses have resulted from sales of IFC investments. These were Rubbertex Proprietary Limited in Australia and Durisol del Peru, S.A., and the two losses amounted to only $391,727.[10] This, however, does not mean that IFC might not incur losses on the sale of other investments in its portfolio.

In addition to these sales from its portfolio, IFC also closed out 22 investments during the period 1956-1966. These terminations amounted to $21.5 million of original IFC commitments made in 12 countries.[11] The yield on these terminations was 12.4 per cent, as compared with an average return on outstanding investments of 6.94 per cent. An analysis of this latter yield reveals that the return on the loan portion was 7.20 per cent and on the equity portion, it was 6.22 per cent.[12]

Finally, IFC has made a number of supplemental commitments to companies which have expanded or which were in need of an infusion of new capital. Approximately one sixth of IFC's total commitments have been additional investments subsequent to an original IFC commitment to these firms. Examples of IFC supplemental investments where expansion of successful ventures was undertaken included Fundidora in Mexico and Arewa Textiles Limited in Nigeria

Miscellaneous Data

The remainder of this section includes tables which set forth a balance sheet for IFC as of June 30, 1966, in Table 21; a comparative statement of income and expenses for the fiscal years 1965 and 1966 in Table 22; and net income for the years during IFC's first decade of operations and the cumulative reserve against losses for the period in Table 23.

EVALUATION

Introduction

Generally, IFC has been quite successful in
fulfilling its objectives during the 1956-1966
period. Taking into consideration the inherent
limitations of financing private enterprise projects in developing countries without government
guarantee--as delineated in Chapter 9, the original
charter limitations prohibiting direct equity participations by IFC, and the former inability to
borrow--impracticable in light of World Bank bor-
rowing--IFC has done a rather noteworthy job in
utilizing its limited capacities.

However, it is quite possible that IFC could
have accomplished more than it did. It is true
that IFC has assisted industrial enterprise projects
whose total cost was $675 million. This amount does
not take into consideration the over $18 million
worth of IFC commitments in DFC's. IFC's net commitment to the industrial projects was $140 million
during its first decade of operations. Thus, for
every IFC dollar invested, other investors contributed about $3.80. The IFC commitments to DFC's
have assisted institutions whose combined portfolios
in 1965 amounted to nearly a half-billion dollars.
Furthermore, during the latter years of the ten-year
period, the trend developed toward more commitments
per year and larger investments per commitment.

However, the analysis of three facets of IFC's
operations suggests that a larger scale of operations might have been possible during the 1956-1966
period. These are: the diversification of IFC commitments by industry, region, and among member nations; the size of IFC investments and total project
cost per company; and a further financial analysis
of such aspects as sale of IFC's investments, its
return on investment, and its reserve against losses.

Table 21

IFC Balance Sheet,
June 30, 1966

ASSETS

Due from Banks		$ 247,731
Investments		
Obligations of		
U.S. Government	$ 48,215,689	
Time Deposits		
Maturing in Less		
Than Six Months	8,500,000	
Accrued Interest	970,383	
		57,686,072
Effective Loans and		
Equity Investments		
Held by IFC		
Loans	55,120,311	
Equity	28,852,885	
		83,973,196
Accrued Income on		
Loans, Equity In-		
vestments and Under-		
writing Commitments		783,553
Receivable from Purchases		
on Account of Effective		
Loans and Equity Invest-		
ments Agreed to be Sold		1,261,042
Other Assets		59,956
Total Assets		$144,011,550

LIABILITIES, RESERVE AND CAPITAL

Liabilities
  Accounts Payable and
    Other Liabilities $ 164,534
  Undisbursed Balance of
    Effective Loans and
    Equity Agreements
      Held by IFC $ 14,498,087
      Agreed to be Sold   1,141,042
                                                  15,639,129

Reserve Against Losses   28,367,887

Capital
  Capital Stock
    Authorized 110,000
      Shares Par Value
      Each $1,000
      Subscribed 99,397 Shares   99,397,000
      Payment on Account of
        Pending Subscription   443,000

    Total Liabilities, Reserve,
      and Capital $144,011,550

Source: IFC, Annual Report 1965-1966 (Washington,
           D.C.: International Finance Corporation,
           1966), p. 30.

Table 22

Comparative Statement of Income and Expenses
For Fiscal Years Ended
June 30, 1965, and June 30, 1966

	1965	1966
INCOME		
Income from Obligations of U.S. Government and Time Deposits	$2,489,886	$2,452,986
Income from Investment Commitments	3,241,837	4,962,112
Other Income	1,196	2,636
GROSS INCOME	$5,732,919	$7,417,734
EXPENSES		
Administrative Expenses:		
Personal services	$1,419,011	$1,605,074
Contributions to staff benefits	209,758	255,241
Fees and compensation	130,025	224,865
Representation	32,080	38,156
Travel	543,109	498,738
Supplies & material	18,639	24,905
Office occupancy	167,435	182,667
Communication services	86,238	90,728
Furniture & equipment	43,579	54,503
Books & library services	22,675	23,753
Printing	41,122	39,928
Insurance	11,035	13,167
Other expenses	801	1,520
	$2,725,507	$3,053,245
NET INCOME – Allocated to Reserve Against Losses	$3,007,412	$4,364,489

Source: IFC, Annual Report 1965-1966 (Washington, D.C.: International Finance Corporation, 1966), p. 31.

Table 23

IFC Net Income,
1956-1966

Year	Net Income	Cumulative Reserve Against Losses
1957	$ 1,675,382	---
1958	2,358,276	---
1959	1,739,757	$ 5,740,965*
1960	2,075,227	7,816,192
1961	2,361,610	10,599,802
1962	2,630,011	13,304,813
1963	3,313,806	17,002,706
1964	2,913,084	20,246,494
1965	3,007,412	23,140,812
1966	4,364,489	28,367,887

*The practice of allocating net income to
a reserve against losses was begun during
fiscal year 1959. Certain other income
has also been allocated to this reserve.

Source: IFC Annual Reports 1956-1966.

Diversification of Investments

First, an analysis of the diversification of
IFC commitments by industry, region, and member
nations shows that, while a fair amount of diversification has been achieved absolutely speaking,
more, perhaps, could have been accomplished. A
relatively few industries have received IFC assistance. Generally, these have been the basic industries such as iron and steel, pulp and paper, and
construction materials. Development advisors have
held that assistance to these industries is necessary in order to achieve higher productivity in
underdeveloped nations. However, there is great
merit in advocating development of the market and
services sectors in LDC's in order to support the
production of basic industries. Marketing channels,
agent middlemen, and facilitating agencies such as
credit and other financial institutions are necessary ingredients in any economic system.

Only through its operations with DFC's has IFC
been able to greatly assist these economic sectors,
and then only indirectly. IFC's investment criteria
generally preclude commitments to enterprises with
less than $500,000 in assets. The DFC's have the
institutional structure to enable their committing
funds to very much smaller projects. However, the
record of DFC's in actually investing in these sectors in amounts much smaller than $50,000 per pro-
ject has not been very good and, thus, they have not
accomplished this important objective which IFC
officials had planned for them.

IFC's commitments by region were concentrated
in Latin America during 1956-1966. This region has
had its Inter-American Development Bank and Alliance
for Progress program during much of this period.
Two thirds of IFC's investments in Latin America
have been concentrated in only four countries,
Brazil, Chile, Colombia, and Mexico.

A further analysis by commitments among member
nations shows that no commitments were made to companies located in twenty-seven member nations as of
June 30, 1966, all of which have relatively very
low per capita incomes.   Ireland, Israel, Kuwait,
and Lebanon are not included among these twenty-
seven nations, nor are sixteen other industrialized
nations which have received no IFC commitments.

This analysis of IFC's investing operations,
coupled with the relatively small percentage of
total project applications approved by IFC, suggests that an investment philosophy somewhat conservative has been advocated by those IFC officials
who pass upon the merits of these applications.
Article III, Section 3 (vii) of IFC's Articles of
Agreement states that "the Corporation shall seek
to maintain a reasonable diversification in its investments." The key word is "reasonable." IFC
officials would certainly insist that reasonable
diversification has been accomplished. However,
the facts show that diversification has been
achieved but that whether it has been reasonable
remains in question. Too much emphasis has been
placed on a few industrial sectors and very little
on the tertiary sector; too much emphasis has been
placed on one region and, until recently, Asia and
Africa have received relatively little IFC assistance; too much IFC emphasis has been placed in too
few member nations at the probable expense of many
others.

On the other hand, logical reasons may exist
for some of these apparent shortcomings. IFC's
early emphasis on Latin American projects stems
from the heavy influence of Latin American support
for an Inter-American Development Bank prior to the
establishment of IFC at a time when the United
States opposed such a development bank. Some World
Bank officials have stated that a favorable atmosphere toward private enterprise existed in Latin
America. However, a similar atmosphere has been
present in other areas of the underdeveloped world
and not all of Latin America has been so favorably
blessed. Perhaps a more valid reason was that

government guarantees to facilitate World Bank project financing were available in most countries but
not in Latin America. Thus, Latin American private
companies had no other resort than to solicit assistance from IFC.

The relatively small number of member countries
which have received IFC investments may not be so
small when the fact is analyzed that several LDC
members do not have good private investment climates
Many of these countries should not be members of IFC
and several will probably never receive IFC assistance. Membership has been obtained with a subscription as little as $2,000 and, thus, many nations
have been able to avail themselves of membership in
IFC.

Size of IFC Investments

The cost of individual projects financed by
IFC as well as IFC commitments per project also
suggest more conservative operations than might
have been possible. The project cost per company
receiving an IFC commitment was approximately $6.75
million when only the industrial projects are considered. IFC's portion per project has averaged
about $1.4 million, after cancellations and termi-
nations have been eliminated. Of the 100 companies
in which IFC has committed funds, thirty-five have
received a commitment totaling less than one million
dollars from IFC. These thirty-five investments in
industrial companies averaged about $468,826.
Therefore, it is possible that IFC could have made
many more smaller, but riskier, investments since
over one third of its commitments were made in
amounts much smaller than its average investment.

However, it should not be overlooked that several of these investments were supplemental where
IFC made a second or third small commitment of funds
in an earlier financed project. Several involved
the exercise of IFC's options to subscribe to stock
made in small rights offerings. Most of these
thirty-five small investments fall into one of these

categories and, thus, distort the average size of
IFC's investments.

IFC has a built-in bias toward large investments because it does not take a managerial interest
in a company it finances nor is it represented on a
company's board of directors. Since there is more
risk in small companies located in less developed
countries, without these safeguards, IFC prefers a
larger project.

Sale of Investments

The sale of its investments represents one of
IFC's principal sources of funds. However, the
profit from such sales is allocated to a reserve
against losses. Since only two losses, totaling
less than $400,000, have been incurred by IFC on
its investments, in addition to the very few cases
where defaults on principal and interest payments
have occurred, the practicability of a reserve
against losses amounting to over $28 million must
be questioned. The net income will continue to
increase as IFC makes more and larger equity investments yielding relatively higher dividend returns,
and thus, the reserve against losses will continue
to grow.

In addition, about half the sales of IFC's investments have been of securities of companies located in only four countries, whereas about 40 per
cent of IFC's portfolio, as of June 30, 1966, was
invested in Argentina, Colombia, India, and Pakistan.
This suggests that IFC may be locked-in from selling
many of these securities because of possible losses.

One high official of IFC has suggested faster
turnover in IFC's portfolio. Surely the reserve
against losses could have covered any losses which
might have occurred and the funds resulting from
those sales could have been used for investment in
higher-yielding equity investments during the last
few years of the 1956-1966 period.

It should be noted, however, that IFC operates
in a manner almost completely opposite that of a
successful investment bank. A good investment bank
holds its most profitable assets as long as possible
and sells losing assets as soon as possible, thus
increasing profits and minimizing losses. IFC sells
its profitable assets as quickly as possible so as
to conform with its objective of increasing the international flow of capital, and it holds losing or
unmarketable securities for long periods of time in
order to season them.

IFC's Return on Investment

The publication of yields ranging over 12 per
cent on the sales of investments by IFC are relatively useless. Naturally, the yield on these sales
will tend to be high because IFC is selling the more
seasoned investments from its portfolio. The current yield on its present portfolio as well as the
current valuation of the portfolio reveal more about
the total operations of IFC. The current yield on
the total portfolio on June 30, 1966, was 6.94 per
cent, including a yield of 6.22 per cent on the
equity portion of the portfolio, a portion amounting
to about one third of the portfolio.

The implication from previous analysis is that
IFC may have a high proportion of its portfolio in
the category labeled "not easily marketable." In
addition to this, the 6.22 per cent yield on equities seems somewhat low for investments in underdeveloped nations. The suggestion is, again, that
IFC's investment operations may be somewhat too
conservative in the light of its original charter
objectives and principles of operations.

CONCLUSIONS

Perhaps IFC could have done more with its limited capacities. Its operations may have been too
conservative and this conservatism may be a reflec-
tion of the predominance of financiers, engineers,
and lawyers among the staff members of IFC.

However, it can be stated with confidence that
IFC has been unique in its operations and that the
organization has more than fulfilled the expectations of even those who testified in favor of such
an institution during congressional or parliamentary hearings in the charter member nations. Some
American officials and Congressmen considered IFC
as being a supplement to the U.S. Export-Import
Bank. Others limited IFC to nonequity participations.

IFC has proved to be a dynamic agent or catalyst in the private enterprise sector of many
countries--directly so in thirty-four of them.
During the period 1956-1966, IFC encouraged directly
or indirectly nearly $4 of investment from other
private interests for every dollar of its own commitments. And what of the additional private enterprise projects financed in these areas merely because IFC assisted one or more companies? How much
financial assistance has been allocated, in a more
economical or profitable way, by local investors or
private foreign financial institutions, in projects
not financed by IFC? IFC's participation in some
projects, in other words, may have permitted other
investors to commit funds in other projects which
were more profitable and more developmental in
their results.

The result of IFC's total operations, therefore, may have resulted in projects costing far
more than the $675 million needed to finance the
100 companies in which IFC invested. As the DFC's
gain more experience, an even more dramatic result
will be seen. The twenty-five such institutions
which have received World Bank Group assistance
have already financed over $1.5 billion in projects.
Thus, if these unknowns were quantifiable, the data
might surely reveal that the establishment of IFC
has resulted in projects in LDC's whose total cost
might amount to, perhaps, billions of dollars.

Another indication of IFC's success can be in-
ferred from the two charter amendments subsequent to
the establishment of IFC. The amendment permitting

equity investments by IFC allowed an expanded level
of operations. The amendment permitting borrowing
by IFC from the World Bank will result in a greatly
expanded capacity of operations. The necessity for
this amendment was the result of IFC's high level of
operations which nearly exhausted its resources.
The equity investment amendment made IFC unique
among development financing institutions and revealed
a high level of confidence in IFC by world leaders.
But what of the future of IFC? Some predictions
about the IFC's future will be the subject of the
final chapter.

11

THE INTERNATIONAL FINANCE CORPORATION: ITS FUTURE

SOME TRENDS

How will IFC operate in the future? Is there
a significant role for IFC to play? Or will other
institutions take its place? During the last few
years, we have witnessed the establishment of a
number of regional development banks including the
Inter-American, Asian and African Development Banks.
At present, some 340 development finance institutions are in existence, several of them predominantly privately owned.[1] What type role will IFC play
when the institutional growth of the development
finance field is considered?

The operations of IFC during the 1966-1967 fiscal year as well as more current operations reveal
some significant trends which facilitate prediction
of the future of IFC. IFC's eleventh fiscal year
was its first full year of operations under the
charter amendment which permitted borrowing from
the World Bank. This amendment, described in Chapter 3, enables IFC to borrow an amount up to four
times its subscribed capital from the Bank, or approximately $400 million. This borrowing is to be
implemented when IFC's undisbursed resources are
reduced to $10 million. A request for $100 million
has already been made. The Bank's standard rate of
interest, presently 6.25 per cent, will be charged
IFC. This borrowing should enable IFC to free its
share capital and reserve against losses, nearly
$134 million, for equity investments.[2]

The 1966-1967 fiscal year was IFC's most active
year of operations. Thirteen commitments totaling
$49.1 million were made.[3] The average size of each
investment was $3.8 million, compared with $1.4 million for the first ten years of IFC operations.
Three investments made ranged in size from $10 to
12 million. Previously, IFC's largest commitments
had been about $6 million. The investments totaling
$49,133,201, were composed of loans amounting to
$33,927,260, and $15,205,941 in equity investments.
An equity position was taken by IFC in all thirteen
commitments.[4]

The total cost of the thirteen projects financed during the year was $330 million. IFC invested
$44.3 million, net of participations, so that for
every dollar invested by IFC, others invested nearly
$6.50. This was the highest ratio of any of the 11
years of IFC financing and the total cost, nearly
half that of the combined total of project costs
1956-1966, was the highest. By the end of the year,
portfolio investments exceeded share capital for
the first time in IFC's history.

An analysis of the new commitments shows that
investments were made for the first time in Kenya
and Senegal, and for the first time to an electric
utility and the tourist industry. 1 These latter
investments were in the Manila Electric Company in
the Philippines and the Kenya Hotel Properties Limited. Small commitments were made to Arewa Textiles
Limited of Nigeria, Fábrica Española Magnetos, S.A.
(FEMSA) in Spain, and Turkiye Sinai Kalkinma Bankasi,
A.S. (TSKB) (The Industrial Development Bank of Turkey), all companies which had received previous IFC
assistance.

Some of the investments were quite small and
represented mostly equity subscriptions. Six of
the thirteen investments, totaling $2,270,232, were
all for amounts less than 1 million dollars and
five of these were equity investments only. The
six commitments averaged less than $400,000; thus
the other seven IFC investments averaged nearly
$6.7 million each.

More rapid growth in IFC interest in Africa
can be seen from 1966-1967 results.   Three commitments totaling $7.2 million were made and two of
these were located in countries receiving an IFC
investment for the first time.   The third was a
supplemental investment in Arewa Textiles Limited,
a Nigerian company whose very successful growth is
analyzed in Chapter 7.

New industry trends can be perceived from the
eleventh year of operations.   The investments in
tourism and an electric utility company have already been mentioned.   The fertilizer industry in
three developing countries further benefited from
IFC commitments.   These were Ultrafértil, S.A., in
Brazil, the Indian Explosives Limited, and Société
Industrielle d'Engrais au Sénégal.   These IFC investments amounted to nearly $25.6 million.[5]

Analysis of the 1966-1967 operations also
shows a possible slowing down in IFC activities in
private development finance companies (DFC's).
Three small commitments were made to DFC's in fiscal year 1966 but only one was made in 1967, and
this was only the exercise of rights to subscribe
to a new issue made by The Industrial Development
Bank of Turkey for $337,500.   This may reflect a
possible saturation of these institutions with international capital,[6] or it may represent a les-
sening of interest in DFC's by IFC because these
institutions have not completely fulfilled IFC's
expectations of them.   They are, for the most part,
still reliant on public funds for their resources
and they generally have not assisted business enterprise whose needs are for project funds in
amounts less than $50,000.

Finally, a trend which seems to be increasing
is the formation of joint venture-type organizations
between IFC, participating private foreign financial
institutions, and local capital on the one hand and
large foreign-controlled multinational corporations
on the other.   This is demonstrated by at least five
of the projects financed by IFC during 1966-1967.

These were:

1. Phillips Petroleum Company of the
    United States in the Ultrafértil,
    S.A., project;

2. Algemene Kunstzijde Unie, N.V. (AKU)
    of the Netherlands in the Enka de
    Colombia, S.A., project;

3. Imperial Chemical Industries of
    England in the Indian Explosives
    Limited project;

4. Pan American World Airways in
    Kenya Hotel Properties Limited;

5. Potasses d'Alsace and Pechiney of
    France in Société Industrielle
    d'Engrais au Sénégal.[7]

Thus larger corporations are becoming interested in
projects submitted to IFC for investments. This
may be attributed to the larger size of IFC investments, in general.

Additional factors which are not present in
the 1966-1967 IFC Annual Report but which should be
mentioned concern operations which have developed
during the present fiscal year, IFC's twelfth. The
first World Bank and IFC financing in Korea took
place when it was announced on February 1, 1968,
that the World Bank would lend $5 million to, and
IFC would subscribe for 14 per cent of the share
capital in, the Korea Development Finance Corporation, a DFC established in 1967 with IFC advisory
assistance. The IFC commitment totaled $713,000.[8]

In addition to this first IFC operation in
Korea, discussions have been taking place recently
between World Bank and IFC officials and Yugoslav-
ian business and government interests. Yugoslavia,
with one of the most liberal business and economic
systems among Communist countries, may be interested
in becoming a member of the International Finance
Corporation.[9]

In addition to the new interest by IFC in Korea and Yugoslavia, a large investment in a fertilizer plant in Pakistan is being considered during 1967-1968. It has been reported that this project will require an IFC commitment of about $25-30 million.[10]

Finally, it is quite clear that the World Bank is placing more and more emphasis on private enterprise by channeling activities to this sector through IFC. The World Bank loans as well as the Bank's delegation to IFC of the responsibility for all World Bank Group industrial project studies and DFC activities are a few of the indicators which add support to this trend.

Thus, recent operations show a number of trends developing or expanding in IFC's operations. Its total investment commitments are growing rapidly each year. The average size of projects receiving IFC approval is increasing rapidly. Growing interest in African development is being maintained and new industries are receiving the attention of IFC. The importance of fertilizer production in less developed countries is being increasingly recognized. Commitments were made for the first time in a number of countries. More and more large multinational corporations are entering into joint investments with IFC.

Will operations similar to these be continued by IFC? What new forms of investment will IFC enter? Will IFC continue to be as successful over the next ten years as it was during its first decade of operations? Are there new directions in which it should move or new opportunities it should study in order to adequately fulfill its charter objectives? Some possible answers to these questions will be discussed in the concluding section.

RECOMMENDATIONS FOR THE FUTURE OF IFC

Intermediate Directions

The future direction of IFC may depend to a great extent on whether certain investment policies of the World Bank are changed. Currently, the World Bank finances some industrial projects. These projects receive Bank loans at the standard rate of interest, currently 6.25 per cent, but these loans are only made with government guarantee. IFC might normally make such loans with interest rates of 8 per cent, but without government guarantees. Thus some project applications may by-pass IFC's higher rate even though some type of government interference might be connected with project financing. In addition, the subsidiary of a multinational corporation may seek World Bank financing because the parent firm may not wish to give up equity in the subsidiary, a prerequisite which IFC will generally require.[11]

Therefore, an increase in feasible project proposals submitted to IFC might result from a change in World Bank policy. In other words, the World Bank might decline any industrial projects which would properly be within the realm of IFC's activities. However, the potential hazard of such a change is that a new policy might result in no project at all and this situation would be opposed to World Bank objectives.

IFC should continue to diversify by country and industry. Many of the developing member nations which have not yet received IFC assistance surely have industrial needs. Naturally, less risk will be desired as IFC's commitments to individual projects enter the $10 million and above category. Thus, private enterprise in the very marginal economies might be more encouraged if IFC could confine some of its activities to these nations, either through direct commitments or through DFC's.

Emphasis on fertilizer production must continue
to be one of IFC's primary objectives. The traditional philosophy in a developing nation toward
having its own complete fertilizer producing facility must be attacked by IFC so that the most economic and productive means of increasing fertilizer
output can be implemented at the lowest cost. This
requires moving raw materials from one or more countries to fertilizer plants located where the optimum means of distribution exists or where local
markets are found.

Tourism and other tertiary service sector industries must receive more assistance from IFC.
Projects such as the hotel being built in Nairobi,
Kenya, will assist the expansion of what is one of
the most important industries in many less developed
nations.

In addition to tourism, financial institutions
are an important part of the economy of many of
these nations. IFC should place more emphasis on
the expansion of insurance companies, consumer loan
companies, mutual funds, and other similar services.
In most developing nations, the financial system is
poorly developed and, thus, private enterprise becomes stifled because of the lack of financing and
farmers and consumers are often at the mercy of
moneylenders. IFC could encourage more investment
by DFC's in smaller amounts per project to companies
in the financial sector. Channeling of IFC funds
in this manner would seem to be a logical course in
developing capital markets and is certainly within
the objectives stated in IFC's charter.

Other IFC operations or policies might be modified in order to expand the reach of the institution. A difference of opinion exists concerning
the sale of IFC's investments. Some think a faster
turnover of investments is possible and necessary.
Certainly more funds would become available for reinvestment. Granted the result might be more losses.
The methods available by which these investments may
be sold place certain limitations on acceleration of
the turnover of IFC's portfolio. A market must be

made for some of the securities and in some countries this is very difficult, especially for un-
seasoned securities of small, little-known companies. There is an indication from IFC's sales of
its investments in recent years that the turnover
is being accelerated. Perhaps it can be accelerated
even more.

Previous analysis suggests that IFC has been
too conservative in some of its investments. With
the increased resources available to IFC from World
Bank borrowing, and with increased profits from
operations and faster turnover of its portfolio,
IFC should accept a higher risk in its investments.
Such a practice would require smaller-than-average
investments as well as the very large commitments
made during recent years. Thus, this shift in
operational policy could lead to increased benefits
in the private sector of developing member nations.

Future Possibilities

At least two potential areas exist in which
IFC might initiate activities in the future. IFC
might consider assisting private enterprise in
packaging complete educational systems for the less
developed nations. Secondly, commitments to private enterprise projects located in underdeveloped
areas of industrialized member nations might be considered by IFC.

Precedents do exist for the investment by private enterprise in packaged education systems. A
number of American companies such as Xerox, Litton
Industries, and RCA have passed through the experi-
mental stage with a number of projects such as programmed learning with teaching machines as well as
contractual arrangements to design, build, and implement whole school systems including building,
equipment, curricula, and instruction. International Telephone and Telegraph Corporation (ITT) and
other companies have contracted with the U.S. government to manage Job Corps Centers under the American poverty programs. IFC has been investigating

the possibility of investing in the educational publishing industry.[12] Many of these projects have
proved to be highly successful ventures although
none are highly profitable and each inherently involves a high amount of risk. However, it seems
that development of education should have high
priority in the developing world and that private
enterprise has proved successful in its investments
in this area.

The second area mentioned, IFC investment commitments to underdeveloped areas in the industrialized countries, would involve a change in IFC philosophy. Such investment is not precluded by the
Articles of Agreement of IFC. In fact, this question was raised during hearings in the U.S. Congress
in 1955 on H.R. 6228, a bill to provide for the participation of the United States in the International
Finance Corporation. U.S. Secretary of the Treasury
George M. Humphrey, in testimony before the House
Committee on Banking and Currency, stated that:
". . . anybody that wants to participate where capital is not available, . . . can present an application."[13] However, one reason for IFC's negative
policy in regard to this type financing may be that
such an investment as a cement plant in Mississippi
would not normally increase the international flow
of private capital and this is one of IFC's principal objectives.

CONCLUSIONS

After describing and analyzing the operations
of the International Finance Corporation, one can
set forth many superlatives and few negative remarks
about the organization. IFC has certainly fulfilled
the original expectations of those who established
it. This unique institution has become a model for
the establishment of regional development banks as
well as private development finance companies in
the underdeveloped areas.

Any organization operating as IFC does and with
its objectives incurs many problems. A learning

process has developed during its first decade of operations and, thus, many of these problems will be eliminated or solved during the second decade of operations.

As new financial resources are developed for IFC, the organization will be able to enter new areas of activity. The peculiar position which IFC occupies in the development of private enterprise facilitates the playing of a far greater role in the emerging new patterns of world economic assistance.

APPENDIX

Statement of Subscriptions

to

Capital Stock and Voting Power

(as of June 30, 1967)

Member	Subscriptions		Voting Power	
	Amount (in thousands of dollars)	Per cent of total	Number of votes	Per cent of total
Afghanistan	$ 111	.11	361	.30
Argentina	1,662	1.66	1,912	1.58
Australia	2,215	2.22	2,465	2.04
Austria	554	.56	804	.67
Belgium	2,492	2.49	2,742	2.27
Bolivia	78	.08	328	.27
Brazil	1,163	1.16	1,413	1.17
Burma	166	.17	416	.34
Canada	3,600	3.60	3,850	3.19
Ceylon	166	.17	416	.34
Chile	388	.39	638	.53
Colombia	388	.39	638	.53
Costa Rica	22	.02	272	.23
Cyprus	83	.08	333	.28
Denmark	753	.75	1,003	.83
Dominican Republic	22	.02	272	.23
Ecuador	35	.04	285	.24
El Salvador	11	.01	261	.22

(continued)

217

Statement of Subscriptions
(Continued)

Member	Subscriptions		Voting Power	
	Amount (in thousands of dollars)	Per cent of total	Number of votes	Per cent of total
Ethiopia	33	.03	283	.23
Finland	421	.42	671	.56
France	5,815	5.82	6,065	5.03
Germany, Federal Republic of	3,655	3.66	3,905	3.24
Ghana	166	.17	416	.34
Greece	277	.28	527	.44
Guatemala	22	.02	272	.23
Guyana	89	.09	339	.28
Haiti	22	.02	272	.23
Honduras	11	.01	261	.22
Iceland	11	.01	261	.22
India	4,431	4.44	4,681	3.88
Iran	372	.37	622	.51
Iraq	67	.07	317	.26
Ireland	332	.33	582	.48
Israel	50	.05	300	.25
Italy	1,994	2.00	2,244	1.86
Ivory Coast	111	.11	361	.30
Jamaica	148	.15	398	.33
Japan	2,769	2.77	3,019	2.50

Jordan	33	.03	283	.23
Kenya	184	.18	434	.36
Korea	139	.14	389	.32
Kuwait	369	.37	619	.51
Lebanon	50	.05	300	.25
Liberia	83	.08	333	.28
Libya	55	.06	305	.25
Luxembourg	111	.11	361	.30
Malagasy Republic	111	.11	361	.30
Malawi	83	.08	333	.28
Malaysia	277	.28	527	.44
Mexico	720	.72	970	.80
Morocco	388	.39	638	.53
Nepal	55	.06	305	.25
Netherlands	3,046	3.05	3,296	2.73
New Zealand	923	.92	1,173	.97
Nicaragua	9	.01	259	.21
Nigeria	369	.37	619	.51
Norway	554	.56	804	.67
Pakistan	1,108	1.11	1,358	1.12
Panama	2	*	252	.21
Paraguay	16	.02	266	.22
Peru	194	.19	444	.37
Philippines	166	.17	416	.34
Portugal	443	.44	693	.57
Saudi Arabia	111	.11	361	.30
Senegal	184	.18	434	.36

(continued)

Statement of Subscriptions
(Continued)

Member	Subscriptions		Voting Power	
	Amount (in thousands of dollars)	Per cent of total	Number of votes	Per cent of total
Sierra Leone	83	.08	333	.28
Somalia	83	.08	333	.28
South Africa	1,108	1.11	1,358	1.12
Spain	1,108	1.11	1,358	1.12
Sudan	111	.11	361	.30
Sweden	1,108	1.11	1,358	1.12
Syrian Arab Republic	72	.07	322	.27
Tanzania	184	.18	434	.36
Thailand	139	.14	389	.32
Togo	83	.08	333	.28
Tunisia	133	.13	383	.32
Turkey	476	.48	726	.60
Uganda	184	.18	434	.36
United Arab Republic	590	.59	840	.70
United Kingdom	14,400	14.41	14,650	12.14
United States	35,168	35.19	35,418	29.35
Venezuela	116	.12	366	.30
Zambia	295	.30	545	.45
TOTALS	$99,929	100.00	120,679	100.00

Source: IFC, Annual Report 1966/1967 (Washington, D.C.: International Finance Corporation, 1967), p. 34.

NOTES

NOTES TO CHAPTER 1

1. "North versus South," an address by U Thant to the Fifth World Conference, Society for International Development, New York, March, 1963.

2. Robert L. Heilbroner, The Great Ascent: The Struggle for Economic Development in our Time (New York: Harper & Row, 1963), pp. 28-30.

3. United Nations, Department of Economic and Social Affairs, The United Nations Development Decade: Proposals for Action (New York: United Nations, 1962), p. 7.

4. Paul G. Hoffmann, World Without Want (New York: Harper & Row, 1962), p. 12.

5. Ibid., p. 19.

6. "International Problems of Economic Development," an address by Irving S. Friedman to the Canadian Political Science Association, Ottawa, Canada, June 7, 1967, p. 1.

7. The United Nations Development Decade, op. cit., p. vi.

8. Heilbroner, op. cit., pp. 14-22.

9. Robert Theobald, The Rich and the Poor: A Study of the Economics of Rising Expectations (New York: The New American Library of World Literature, 1960), p. 12.

10. James M. Burns and Jack W. Peltason, Government By The People (Englewood Cliffs, N.J.: Prentice-Hall, Inc., 1957), pp. 607-609.

11. Ibid., p. 610.

12. The World Bank Group at Work (Washington, D.C.: International Bank for Reconstruction and Development, 1967), p. 1.

13. Ibid.

14. Ibid.

15. Wolfgang G. Friedmann, George Kalmanoff, and Robert F. Meagher, International Financial Aid (New York: Columbia University Press, 1966), pp. 46-54.

16. Guenther Riemann, "Foreign Financing of the Underdeveloped Countries," in Guenther Riemann and Edwin F. Wigglesworth (eds.), The Challenge of International Finance (New York: McGraw-Hill, 1966), p. 147.

17. David Rockefeller, "The Case for Foreign Aid," World Business (May, 1967), p. 6.

18. "International Outlook," Business Week, No. 1998 (December 23, 1967), p. 62.

19. Friedmann, Kalmanoff, and Meagher, op. cit., p. 52.

20. Proposed Foreign Aid Program FY 1968 (Washington, D.C.: Agency for International Development, 1967)--Summary Presentation to the Congress, p. 4.

21. The Foreign Assistance Program, Annual Report to the Congress FY 1966 (Washington, D.C.: Agency for International Development, 1968), p. 10, and The Foreign Assistance Program, Annual Report to the Congress, FY 1967 (Washington, D.C.: Agency for International Development, 1968), p. 13.

22. The Foreign Assistance Program, FY 1967, op. cit.

23. Riemann and Wigglesworth, op. cit., p. 147.

24. _Ibid._

25. _Ibid._

26. Andrew J. Glass, "... and Now to the Bank,"
The New Republic, Vol. 158 (February 17, 1968),
22-23.

27. _The United Nations Development Decade_,
op. cit., p. vii.

28. David Rockefeller, "The Case for Foreign
Aid," _op. cit._, p. 9.

29. Glass, "... and Now to the Bank," _op. cit._,
p. 22.

30. From a presentation by John Adler, Economic
Development Institute, International Bank for Reconstruction and Development, at the Annual World Conference, Society for International Development, in
Washington, D.C., March 9, 1968.

31. From a presentation at the Annual World
Conference, Society for International Development,
in Washington, D.C., March 9, 1968.

32. "International Outlook," _Business Week_,
op. cit.

33. _The World Bank Group at Work_, _op. cit._

34. Background material for this section was
derived from "Development--The Need for New Directions," an address by George D. Woods, President,
World Bank Group, to The Swedish Bankers Association, Stockholm, October 27, 1967.

35. "Private Investment in the Developing
Countries," an address by Martin M. Rosen, Executive
Vice President, IFC, to the National Convocation on
World Hunger, National Industrial Conference Board,
New York, September 12, 1967, p. 2.

36.   From a presentation before the Annual World Conference, Society for International Development, op. cit.

37.   A Richer Harvest: A Report on Ford Foundation Grants in Overseas Agriculture (New York: Ford Foundation, 1967); The United States Food and Fiber System in a Changing World Environment (Washington, D.C.: National Advisory Commission on Food and Fiber, 1967); Simon Williams, "Private Investment in World Agriculture," Harvard Business Review, Vol. 43 (November-December, 1965), 99-105; Ray A. Goldberg, "Agribusiness for Developing Countries," Harvard Business Review, Vol. 44 (September-October, 1966), 81-93.

38.   "The Green Revolution: Accomplishments and Apprehensions," an address by William S. Gaud, Administrator, U.S. Agency for International Development, given before the Society for International Development, Washington, D.C., March 8, 1968.

39.   Rosen, "Private Investment in the Developing Countries," op. cit., p. 11.

40.   Ibid.

41.   Ibid., p. 12.

42.   "Financing Fertilizer Production in the Developing Countries," an address by Martin M. Rosen, Executive Vice President, IFC, at the First International Agribusiness Conference, Chicago, May 10, 1967, p. 2.

43.   Rosen, "Private Investment in Developing Countries," op. cit., p. 13.

44.   "The Role of International Agencies in Aiding World Food Production," an address by J. Burke Knapp, Vice President, World Bank, to the National Academy of Science's Scientific Program, Washington, D.C., April 25, 1966.

45.   Rosen, "Financing Fertilizer Production in the Developing Countries," op. cit., p. 3.

46.   Ibid.

47.   Ibid., p. 4.

48.   Gaud, "The Green Revolution...," op. cit.

49.   Ibid., p. 5.

NOTES TO CHAPTER 2

1.   U.S., Congress, House, Committee on Foreign Affairs, Staff Memorandum on International Lending Agencies. 87th Cong., 1st Sess., 1961, p. 1.

2.   B. E. Matecki, Establishment of the International Finance Corporation and United States Policy. (New York: Frederick A. Praeger, Inc., 1957), pp. 49-51.

3.   Ibid., p. 32.

4.   U.N. Economic and Social Council, Document E/1245/Revision 1 of May 3, 1947.

5.   Matecki, op. cit., p. 79.

6.   U.S., Congress, House, Report No. 1299 of July 20, 1955, 84th Cong., 1st Sess., 1955, p. 3, as well as Hearings before the Committee on Banking and Currency, House of Representative, 84th Cong., 1st Sess., on H.R. 6228, A Bill to Establish the International Finance Corporation, July 11 & 14, 1955.

7.   U.N., ECOSOC, Document E/2441 of May 25, 1953.

8.   U.N., ECOSOC, Document E/2616 of June 3, 1954.

9.   Matecki, op. cit., p. 126.

10. "U.S. for New Body on Overseas Help," _The New York Times_, November 12, 1954.

11. International Bank for Reconstruction and Development, _The Proposed International Finance Corporation_ (Washington, D.C.: International Bank for Reconstruction and Development, May, 1955), p. 6

12. H.R. _Report No. 1299_, op. cit., pp. 2-3.

13. U.S., Congress, Senate, _Hearings before a Subcommittee of the Committee on Banking and Currency on S. 1894_, 84th Cong., 1st Sess., June 6 & 7, 1955, p. 15.

14. _Ibid._, p. 28.

15. _Ibid._, p. 110.

16. U.S. Congress, _International Finance Corporation Act_, Public Law 350, 84th Cong., 1st Sess., Statute 669, approved August 11, 1955.

17. Matecki, op. cit., Chapter 7.

NOTES TO CHAPTER 3

1. Article I, _Articles of Agreement of the International Finance Corporation_, Washington, D.C., July 20, 1956, p. 3.

2. _Ibid._, pp. 3-4.

3. U.S., Congress, Senate, _Report No. 505 of June 10, 1955_, 84th Cong., 1st Sess., p. 5.

4. Article II, _Articles of Agreement_, op. cit. pp. 4-5.

5. International Finance Corporation, _First Annual Report 1956-1957_ (Washington, D.C.: International Finance Corporation, 1957), p. 5.

6. International Financial News Survey, Vol. 19
(January 13, 1967), 7.

7. National Advisory Council, The Eighth
Special Report of the National Advisory Council on
International Monetary and Financial Problems,
House Document No. 175, 88th Cong., 1st Sess.
(Washington, D.C.: U.S. Government Printing Office,
November 25, 1963), p. 30.

8. IFC, Annual Report 1965-1966 (Washington,
D.C.: International Finance Corporation, 1966),
p. 7.

9. Article III, Section 3, paragraph vi,
Articles of Agreement, op. cit., p. 7.

10. IFC, Annual Report 1965-1966, op. cit.,
p. 12.

11. Ibid.

12. Ibid.

13. Ibid., p. 31.

14. Article III, Section 6, paragraph i,
Articles of Agreement, op. cit., p. 7.

15. Summary Proceedings, 1964 Annual Meeting
of the Board of Governors (Washington, D.C.: International Finance Corporation, October 31, 1964),
pp. 14-20.

16. Article III, Section 3, Articles of Agreement, op. cit., p. 9.

17. IFC, Annual Report 1965-1966, op. cit.,
p. 8.

18. U.S., Congress, House, Committee on Foreign
Affairs, Staff Memorandum on International Lending
Agencies, 87th Cong., 1st Sess., 1961, p. 3.

19. Hearings before Subcommittee No. 1 of the House Committee on Banking and Currency on H.R. 6765 87th Cong., 1st Sess., May 10, 1961, p. 3.

20. IFC, Sixth Annual Report 1961-1962 (Washington, D.C.: International Finance Corporation, 1962), p. 13.

21. IFC, Annual Report 1965-1966, op. cit., pp. 8-9.

22. Ibid., p. 9.

23. M. M. Mendels, "IFC: investment banker to world free enterprise," Industrial Canada, June, 1966, p. 2.

24. IFC, Annual Report 1965-1966, op. cit., p. 10.

25. IFC, Sixth Annual Report 1961-1962, op. cit pp. 10-11.

26. Shirley Boskey, Problems and Practices of Development Banks (Baltimore, Md.: The Johns Hopkins Press, 1959), pp. 3-4. Other background material for this section was derived from an interview with William Diamond, Director, IFC's Development Finance Companies Department, in Washington, D.C., February 14, 1968.

27. Private Development Finance Companies (Washington, D.C.: International Finance Corporation, 1964), p. 3.

28. Ibid., p. 9.

29. "Some Aspects of Policy and Operation of Development Finance Companies," an unpublished manuscript of essays by E.T. Kuiper, Douglas Gustafson, and P.M. Mathew, of the International Finance Corporation, 1967, p. 17 (mimeographed).

30. Ibid., pp. 17-18.

31.   Ibid., p. 24.

32.   Ibid., pp. 40-71.

33.   The Role of National Development Finance Companies in Industrial Development, (An Information Paper prepared by the World Bank Group for the International Symposium on Industrial Development sponsored by the United Nations Industrial Development Organization, Athens, Greece, December, 1967), p. 2.

34.   IFC, Sixth Annual Report, 1961-1962, op. cit., p. 9.

35.   IFC, Seventh Annual Report, 1962-1963 (Washington, D.C.:   International Finance Corporation, 1963), p. 6.

36.   William L. Bennet, "Developing Private Enterprise Internationally," Commerce, Vol. 62 (March, 1965), 9-10.

37.   IFC, Seventh Annual Report, 1962-1963, op. cit., p. 21.

38.   IFC, Eighth Annual Report, 1963-1964 (Washington, D.C.:   International Finance Corporation, 1964), p. 9.

39.   IFC, Annual Report, 1964-1965 (Washington, D.C.:   International Finance Corporation, 1965), p. 11.

NOTES TO CHAPTER 4

1.   From "Industrial Promotion," an address by Martin M. Rosen, Executive Vice President, IFC, at the First International Meeting of Financial Institutions for Development, Caracas, Venezuela, February 18, 1964.

2. From an interview with Judhvir Parmar, Investment Officer of IFC, at IFC Washington, January 18, 1967.

3. Ibid.

4. From an interview with James S. Raj, Vice President, International Finance Corporation, in Washington, D.C., February 23, 1968.

5. Ibid.

6. E.E. Halmos, Jr., "The IFC's engineering department," Worldwide P&I Planning, Vol. 1 (September/October, 1967), 52.

7. Interview with James S. Raj, op. cit.

8. International Finance Corporation, Annual Report 1965-1966 (Washington, D.C.: International Finance Corporation, 1966), p. 9.

9. IFC, Eighth Annual Report 1963-1964 (Washington, D.C.: International Finance Corporation, 1964), p. 10.

10. Interview with James S. Raj, op. cit.

11. Halmos, op. cit., p. 55.

12. IFC, Second Annual Report 1957-1958 (Washington, D.C.: International Finance Corporation, 1958), p. 6.

13. Ibid., p. 7.

14. Accounting and Financial Reporting (Washington, D.C.: International Finance Corporation, August, 1964), pp. 1-4.

15. Ibid., pp. 4-8.

16. Accounting..., op. cit., pp. 8-11.

17. From the Rosen address in Caracas, Venezuela, op. cit.

18. Ibid.

19. From an interview with Donald C. Eynon,
IFC Investment Officer, in Washington, D.C.,
February 14, 1968.

NOTES TO CHAPTER 5

1. "The World Bank Group in Latin America,"
an address by Orvis A. Schmidt, before the Canadian
Inter-American Association, Montreal, Canada,
March 2, 1966.

2. International Finance Corporation, Annual
Report 1965-1966 (Washington, D.C.: International
Finance Corporation, 1966), pp. 32, 34, 36, and 38.

3. IFC, Annual Report 1964-1965 (Washington,
D.C.: International Finance Corporation, 1965),
p. 9.

4. Ibid.

5. IFC, Seventh Annual Report 1962-1963 (Washington, D.C.: International Finance Corporation,
1963), p. 7.

6. Reader's Digest 1967 Almanac and Yearbook
(Pleasantville, N.Y.: The Reader's Digest Association, Inc., 1967), p. 813.

7. International Finance Corporation Press
Release No. 34, September 28, 1959, p. 1.

8. Ibid.

9. Ibid.

10. From correspondence received from FERTISA,
dated August 29, 1967.

11.   IFC, Fourth Annual Report 1959-1960 (Washington, D.C.:   International Finance Corporation, 1960), p. 18.

12.   IFC, Sixth Annual Report 1961-1962 (Washington, D.C.:   International Finance Corporation, 1962), p. 12.

13.   Ibid., pp. 12-13.

14.   IFC, Annual Report 1965-1966, op. cit., p. 16.

15.   IFC, Annual Report 1966/1967 (Washington, D.C.:   International Finance Corporation, 1967), p. 9.

16.   Memoria y Balance General al 31 de Diciembre de 1966 (Lima, Peru: Fertilizantes Sinteticos S.A. (FERTISA), p. 3.

17.   Ibid.

18.   Ibid.

19.   Ibid.

20.   Ibid., p. 4.

21.   International Bank for Reconstruction and Development, The World Bank Group in the Americas (Washington, D.C.:   International Bank for Reconstruction and Development, 1963), p. 85.

22.   Material for this section came from: Reader's Digest 1967 Almanac and Yearbook, op. cit., pp. 681-682.

23.   John G. McLean, "Financing Overseas Expansion," Harvard Business Review, XLI (March-April, 1963), 61.

24.   Ibid.

25. The World Bank Group in the Americas,
op. cit., p. 85.

26. Chase Manhattan Bank Press Release,
October 11, 1961, p. 2.

27. McLean, op. cit., p. 61.

28. IFC, Sixth Annual Report 1961-1962,
op. cit., p. 8.

29. McLean, op. cit., p. 63.

30. Chase Manhattan Bank Press Release,
op. cit., p. 1.

31. McLean, op. cit., p. 64.

32. Ibid., p. 65.

33. Ibid.

34. The World Bank Group in Mexico (Washington,
D.C.: International Bank for Reconstruction and
Development, 1967); other data from Reader's Digest
1967 Almanac and Yearbook, op. cit., pp. 794, 796.

35. The World Bank Group in Mexico, op. cit.,
pp. 1-2.

36. Ibid., p. 2.

37. Ibid., p. 11.

38. "Cia. Fundidora de Fierro y Acero de
Monterrey, S.A., Mexico," a publication furnished
by Fundidora company officials, dated November,
1960, p. 2.

39. Ibid., p. 3.

40. Ibid.

41. Ibid.

42. IFC, <u>Sixth Annual Report 1961-1962</u>, <u>op. cit</u>., p. 10.

43. IFC Press Release No. 62/6, June 19, 1962, p. 2.

44. <u>Ibid</u>.

45. IFC, <u>Sixth Annual Report 1961-1962</u>, <u>op. cit</u>., p. 11.

46. IFC Press Release No. 64/14, August 22, 1964, pp. 1-2.

47. IFC, <u>Annual Report 1964-1965</u>, <u>op. cit</u>., p. 16.

48. IFC Press Release No. 66/9, May 31, 1966, p. 1.

49. <u>Ibid</u>.

50. IFC, <u>Annual Report 1965-1966</u>, <u>op. cit</u>., pp. 24-25.

51. <u>Ibid</u>., p. 25.

52. <u>Ibid</u>., p. 37.

53. <u>Annual Report Fiscal Year 1965</u> (Monterrey, Mexico: Compañia Fundidora de Fierro y Acero de Monterrey, S.A., 1965), p. 4.

54. <u>Ibid</u>.

55. <u>Ibid</u>., p. 5.

56. <u>The Ross Report of Investor's Mexican Letter</u>, an advisory business service, XI, No. 8, April 20, 1967, 2.

57. <u>Ibid</u>.

58. <u>Annual Report Fiscal Year 1965</u>, <u>op. cit</u>., p. 7.

59. David Grenier, "IFC: An Expanded Role for Venture Capital," Finance and Development, IV (June, 1967), 139.

60. The World Bank Group in Brazil (Washington, D.C.: International Bank for Reconstruction and Development, 1967).

61. Ibid., p. 1.

62. Ibid., p. 2.

63. IFC Press Release No. 65/13, December 7, 1965, pp. 1-2.

64. IFC, Annual Report 1965-1966, op. cit., p. 19.

65. IFC Press Release, December 7, 1965, op. cit., p. 1.

66. Ibid.

67. From a conversation with Frank Lamson-Scribner, an IFC Loan Officer, October 26, 1967.

68. IFC Press Release No. 66/7, May 21, 1966, pp. 1-2.

69. IFC, Annual Report 1965-1966, op. cit., p. 19.

70. IFC Press Release No. 66/7, op. cit., p. 3.

71. Notes from correspondence received from A.C. Lobl, a director of Papel e Celulose, S.A., August 22, 1967.

72. Ibid.

73. Ibid.

74. Ibid.

75. IFC Press Release No. 66/7, op. cit.,
pp. 2-3.

76. Ibid.

77. IFC, Annual Report 1965-1966, op. cit.,
pp. 32, 38.

78. IFC Press Release No. 60, September 8,
1961, p. 1.

79. Ibid.

80. IFC, Sixth Annual Report 1961-1962, op.
cit., p. 9.

81. IFC News Release No. 67/7, September 28,
1967, pp. 1-2.

82. IFC, Eighth Annual Report 1963-1964
(Washington, D.C.: International Finance Corporation, 1964), p. 37.

83. IFC News Release No. 67/7, op. cit., p. 2.

84. The Role of National Development Finance
Companies in Industrial Development, an information
paper prepared by the World Bank Group for the
International Symposium on Industrial Development
sponsored by the United Nations Industrial Development Organization, Athens, Greece, December, 1967,
p. 20.

85. IFC News Release No. 67/7, op. cit., p. 2.

86. IFC Press Release No. 64/7, April 1, 1964,
p. 1.

87. IFC, Eighth Annual Report 1963-1964,
op. cit., p. 17.

88. Ibid.

NOTES TO CHAPTER 6

1.   International Finance Corporation, <u>Annual
Report 1965-1966</u> (Washington, D.C.:   International
Finance Corporation, 1966), p. 4.

2.   The data for this section was derived from
various annual reports published by IFC; Press Releases No. 61, dated September 15, 1961, No. 64,
dated December 28, 1961, and No. 65/6, dated May 26,
1965; and <u>Annual Report of Ismail Cement Industries
Limited Ismailwal</u>, for the period ended 30th June,
1966.

3.   IFC Press Release No. 64, December 28,
1961, p. 2.

4.   <u>Annual Report of Ismail Cement Industries
Limited</u>, <u>op. cit.</u>, p. 4.

5.   IFC Press Release No. 64/2, January 6,
1964, p. 3.

6.   "Mahindra Ugine Steel Company," <u>Monthly
Newsletter of the Indian Investment Centre</u>, V,
(February 15, 1968), 6.

7.   Derived from correspondence from P.O.
Mistry, Secretary, MUSCO, written July 13, 1967.

8.   <u>Annual Report and Accounts 1966</u> (Bombay:
Mahindra Ugine Steel Company, Ltd., 1967), pp. 7-8.

9.   "Mahindra Ugine Steel Company," <u>op. cit.</u>,
p. 6.

10.   <u>Ibid</u>.

11.   IFC Press Release No. 65/7, June 23, 1965,
pp. 1-2.

12.   IFC, <u>Annual Report 1964-1965</u> (Washington,
D.C.:   International Finance Corporation, 1965), p. 18.

13. Packages Limited, Annual Report 1966 (Lahore, West Pakistan: Packages, Ltd., 1967).

14. Correspondence from Syed Irshad Hussain, Director and General Manager, Packages, Ltd., sent June 10, 1967.

15. IFC, Seventh Annual Report 1962-1963 (Washington, D.C.: International Finance Corporation, 1963), pp. 18-19.

16. "Some Aspects of Policy and Operation of Development Finance Companies," an unpublished manuscript of essays by E.T. Kuiper, Douglas Gustafson, and P.M. Mathew, of the International Finance Corporation, pp. 56-57.

17. IFC, Seventh Annual Report 1962-1963, op. cit., pp. 19-21.

18. "IFC and the Growing Need for Private Investment in the Low Income Countries," an address by Martin M. Rosen, Executive Vice President, IFC, to the Seminar on International Development, York University School of Business, Toronto, Canada, November 7, 1967.

19. "Some Aspects of Policy and Operation of Development Finance Companies," op. cit., p. 60.

20. IFC, Eighth Annual Report 1963-1964 (Washington, D.C.: International Finance Corporation, 1964), p. 25.

21. The Role of National Development Finance Companies in Industrial Development, an information paper prepared by the World Bank Group for the International Symposium on Industrial Development sponsored by the United Nations Industrial Development Organization, Athens, Greece, December, 1967, pp. 12-13.

22. IFC, Eighth Annual Report 1963-1964, op. cit., p. 35.

NOTES TO CHAPTER 7

1. _The World Bank Group in Africa_ (Washington, D.C.: International Bank for Reconstruction and Development, 1963), p. 1.

2. _Ibid._

3. International Finance Corporation, _Annual Report 1965-1966_ (Washington, D.C.: International Finance Corporation, 1966), p. 4.

4. International Finance Corporation Press Release No. 38, June 3, 1960, pp. 1-2.

5. _Ibid._, p. 1

6. _Ibid._

7. Kilombero Sugar Company Limited, _Annual Report 1965/1966_, p. 5.

8. _Ibid._

9. _The World Bank Group in Tunisia_ (Washington, D.C.: International Bank for Reconstruction and Development, 1967), p. 1.

10. IFC Press Release No. 62/9, November 9, 1962, p. 3.

11. Martin M. Rosen, "International Finance Corporation: Its Policies and Operations," _European Business Review_ (September, 1965), p. 6.

12. M.M. Mendels, "IFC: investment banker to world free enterprise," _Industrial Canada_ (June, 1966), p. 3.

13. IFC, _Seventh Annual Report 1962-1963_ (Washington, D.C.: International Finance Corporation, 1963), p. 22.

14.   IFC Press Release No. 62/9, op. cit., p. 2, and IFC, Seventh Annual Report 1962-1963, op. cit., p. 22.

15.   The United Nations and the Business World (New York: Business International, 1967), p. 76.

16.   IFC, Annual Report 1964-1965 (Washington, D.C.: International Finance Corporation, 1965), p. 14.

17.   Ibid., p. 14.

18.   Cotton Company of Ethiopia, Report for the Year Ended 31st May 1967, p. 14.

19.   IFC Press Release No. 64/18, October 8, 1964, p. 1.

20.   Cotton Company, Report for the Year..., op. cit., p. 15.

21.   Reader's Digest 1967 Almanac and Yearbook (Pleasantville, New York: The Reader's Digest Association, Inc., 1966), p. 845.

22.   IFC Press Release No. 65/5, May 12, 1965, p. 1.

23.   Ibid., p. 2.

24.   Ibid.

25.   "East Africa Rejoices in New Union," Uganda Argus, December 2, 1967, p. 1.

26.   "Next Ethiopia and Zambia," Uganda Argus, December 4, 1967, p. 1.

27.   "Boosting Home Industry," Uganda Argus, December 5, 1967, p. 1.

28.   "Transfer tax welcomed," Uganda Argus, December 6, 1967, p. 11.

29.   Some of the background information on the
IFC-Mulco investment was derived from an interview
with Donald Eynon, Investment Officer, International Finance Corporation, Washington, D.C.,
October 26, 1967.

30.   Reader's Digest 1967 Almanac and Yearbook,
op. cit., pp. 806-807.

31.   IFC Press Release No. 64/3, January 16,
1964, p. 1.

32.   IFC, Eighth Annual Report 1963-1964
(Washington, D.C.:   International Finance Corporation, 1964), p. 27.

33.   IFC Press Release No. 67/1, February 24,
1967, p. 1.

34.   IFC, Annual Report 1966/1967 (Washington,
D.C.:   International Finance Corporation, 1967),
p. 15.

35.   Ibid.

36.   Background material for the IFC-Arewa in-
vestment was derived from an interview with Donald
Eynon, Investment Officer, International Finance
Corporation, Washington, D.C., October 26, 1967,
and an address by Martin M. Rosen, Executive Vice
President, IFC, to the Seminar on International
Development, York University School of Business,
Toronto, Canada, November 7, 1967, entitled "IFC
and the Growing Need for Private Investment in the
Low Income Countries."

37.   IFC, Seventh Annual Report 1962-1963,
op. cit., p. 17.

38.   Ibid., p. 18.

39.   IFC, Eighth Annual Report 1963-1964,
op. cit., p. 30.

40.   Ibid.

41. "Some Aspects of Policy and Operation of Development Finance Companies," an unpublished manuscript of essays by E.T. Kuiper, Douglas Gustafson, and P.M. Mathew, of the International Finance Corporation, pp. 57, 68.

42. IFC, Annual Report 1964-1965, op. cit., p. 16.

43. IFC, Annual Report 1965-1966 (Washington, D.C.: International Finance Corporation, 1966), p. 23.

44. From a conversation with William Diamond, Director, Development Finance Companies Department, International Finance Corporation, Washington, D.C. February 14, 1968.

45. IFC, Annual Report 1965-1966, op. cit., p. 24.

46. Ibid., p. 26.

47. Ibid.

NOTES TO CHAPTER 8

1. Reader's Digest 1967 Almanac and Yearbook (Pleasantville, N.Y.: The Reader's Digest Association, 1966), p. 747.

2. From the Fifty-Sixth Annual Report of General Cement Company, S.A., for the year ended December 31, 1966, and Annual Report for the Year 1966 for "Titan" Cement Company, S.A.

3. International Finance Corporation Press Release No. 66/3, April 1, 1966, p. 2.

4. Ibid.

5. International Finance Corporation, Annual Report 1965-1966 (Washington, D.C.: International Finance Corporation, 1966), p. 22.

6.   Ibid.

7.   Ibid., p. 23.

8.   Fifty-Sixth Annual Report of General
Cement Company, op. cit., p. 11.

9.   Ibid., p. 10.

10.   Background material for this case study
was also obtained from interviews with Ernesto
Franco, IFC European Investment Officer, and
Chauncey Dewey and Peter Muth, IFC Investment Officers, in Washington, D.C., February 16, 1968.

11.   Reader's Digest 1967 Almanac and Yearbook,
op. cit., p. 830.

12.   Ibid., p. 831.

13.   World Bank and IDA Annual Report 1966/1967
(Washington, D.C.:   International Bank for Reconstruction and Development and International Development Association, 1967), p. 69.

14.   Fábrica Expañola Magnetos S.A., Esto es
FEMSA (Madrid, Spain: Fábrica Española Magnetos
S.A., March, 1967), p. 3.

15.   IFC, Sixth Annual Report 1961-1962 (Washington, D.C.:   International Finance Corporation,
1962), p. 13.

16.   IFC Press Release No. 62/4, February 28,
1962, p. 2.

17.   IFC, Sixth Annual Report, op. cit., p. 13.

18.   IFC Press Release No. 64/17, September 23,
1964, p. 2.

19.   Ibid.

20.   IFC, Annual Report 1964-1965 (Washington,
D.C.:   International Finance Corporation, 1965), p. 19.

21. IFC Press Release No. 66/13, September 14, 1966, p. 2.

22. Ibid.

23. Esto es FEMSA, op. cit., pp. 25, 27, 29, 31.

24. IFC, Eighth Annual Report 1963-1964 (Washington, D.C.: International Finance Corporation, 1964), p. 19.

25. Ibid., p. 18-19.

26. The Role of National Development Finance Companies in Industrial Development (An Information Paper prepared by the World Bank Group for the International Symposium on Industrial Development sponsored by the United Nations Industrial Development Organization, Athens, Greece, December, 1967), p. 16.

27. Ibid., p. 20.

28. Ibid., p. 36.

29. Ibid., pp. 36-37.

30. Ibid., p. 19.

31. "Some Aspects of Policy and Operation of Development Finance Companies," an unpublished manuscript of essays by E.T. Kuiper, Douglas Gustafson, and P.M. Mathew, of the International Finance Corporation, pp. 103-104.

32. IFC, Seventh Annual Report 1962-1963 (Washington, D.C.: International Finance Corporation, 1963), p. 21.

33. The Role of National Development Finance Companies..., op. cit., p. 19.

34. IFC, Eighth Annual Report 1963-1964, op. cit., pp. 18-19.

35.   Ibid., p. 19.

36.   IFC, Annual Report 1965-1966, op. cit.,
p. 22.

37.   Ibid.

38.   The Role of National Development Finance
Companies..., op. cit., pp. 13, 16.

NOTES TO CHAPTER 9

1.   From correspondence dated February 19,
1968, from Dr. Hermann J. Abs, a member of IFC's
international advisory panel.

2.   Maneck S. Wadia, "The Concept of Culture,"
Journal of Retailing, XLI (Spring, 1965), 55.

3.   Edward T. Hall, The Silent Language (New
York: Doubleday, 1959).

4.   James A. Lee, "Cultural Analysis in Overseas Operations," Harvard Business Review, XLIV
(March-April, 1966), 106.

5.   Correspondence from Dr. Hermann J. Abs,
op. cit.

6.   International Finance Corporation, Third
Annual Report 1958-1959 (Washington, D.C.: International Finance Corporation, 1959), p. 4.

7.   The Second Five-year Plan for Development
of Science and Technology, 1967-1971 (Seoul: Government of the Republic of Korea, July, 1966).

8.   IFC, Fourth Annual Report 1959-1960 (Washington, D.C.: International Finance Corporation,
1960), p. 5.

9.   See Chapter 7.

10. See Chapter 7.

11. See Chapter 6.

12. IFC, Fourth Annual Report, op. cit., p. 8.

13. Charles K. Laurent and Aquileo Parra A.,
"Use of Mail Questionnaires in Colombia," Journal
of Marketing Research, V (February, 1968), 101.

14. IFC, Fifth Annual Report 1960-1961 (Washington, D.C.: International Finance Corporation,
1961), p. 6.

15. Ibid.

16. See Chapter 5.

17. See Chapter 7.

18. IFC, Second Annual Report 1957-1958 (Washington, D.C.: International Finance Corporation,
1958), p. 6.

19. See Chapter 5.

20. See Chapter 5.

21. "Industrial Promotion," an address by
Martin M. Rosen, Executive Vice President, IFC, at
the First International Meeting of Financial Institutions for Development, Caracas, Venezuela,
February 18, 1964, p. 15.

NOTES TO CHAPTER 10

1. International Finance Corporation, Annual
Report 1965-1966 (Washington, D.C.: International
Finance Corporation, 1966), p. 7.

2. Ibid., p. 4.

3. Ibid., p. 41.

4.   See Chapter 5.

5.   IFC, <u>Annual Report 1965-1966</u>, <u>op. cit.</u>,
p. 11.

6.   <u>The United Nations & the Business World</u>
(New York: Business International, 1967), pp. 77-78.

7.   J.D. Nyhart and Edmond F. Janssens, <u>A</u>
<u>Global Directory of Development Finance Institutions</u>
<u>in Developing Countries</u> (Paris: The Development
Centre of the Organisation for Economic Co-operation
and Development, 1967).

8.   IFC, <u>Annual Report 1965-1966</u>, <u>op. cit.</u>,
p. 12.

9.   <u>Ibid.</u>, pp. 8-9.

10.   IFC, <u>Eighth Annual Report 1963-1964</u> (Washington, D.C.:   International Finance Corporation,
1964), p. 13, and IFC, <u>Annual Report 1965-1966</u>,
<u>op. cit.</u>, p. 12.

11.   IFC, <u>Annual Report 1965-1966</u>, <u>op. cit.</u>,
p. 12.

12.   <u>Ibid.</u>

NOTES TO CHAPTER 11

1.   J.D. Nyhart and Edmond F. Janssens, <u>A</u>
<u>Global Directory of Development Finance Institutions</u>
<u>in Developing Countries</u> (Paris: The Development
Centre of the Organisation for Economic Co-operation
and Development, 1967).

2.   International Finance Corporation, <u>Annual</u>
<u>Report 1965-1966</u> (Washington, D.C.:   International
Finance Corporation, 1966), p. 13.

3.   IFC, <u>Annual Report 1966/1967</u> (Washington,
D.C.:   International Finance Corporation, 1967), p. 5.

4. _Ibid._, p. 11.

5. _Ibid._, pp. 12, 14, 16-17.

6. The United Nations & the Business World (New York: Business International, 1967), p. 78.

7. _Ibid._, p. 75.

8. IFC Press Release No. 68/1, February 1, 196

9. From numerous conversations with IFC officials during 1967-1968.

10. Interview with James S. Raj, Vice President IFC, in Washington, D.C., February 23, 1968.

11. _Ibid._

12. From an interview with Martin M. Rosen, Executive Vice President, IFC, in Washington, D.C., April 17, 1968.

13. U.S., Congress, House, Hearings before the Committee on Banking and Currency on H.R. 6228, A Bill to Establish the International Finance Corporation, 84th Cong., 1st Sess., July 11 and 14, 1955.

BIBLIOGRAPHY

BIBLIOGRAPHY

Public Documents

Gray, Gordon. Report to the President on Foreign
Economic Policies. Washington, D.C.: U.S.
Government Printing Office, 1950.

Partners in Progress. A Report to the President by
the International Development Advisory Board.
Washington, D.C.: U.S. Government Printing
Office, 1951.

U.S. House of Representatives, Committee on Banking
and Currency. Hearings on H.R. 6228, A Bill
to Establish the International Finance Corporation. 84th Congress, 1st Session, 1955.

_____, Committee on Foreign Affairs. Staff Memo-
randum on International Lending Agencies.
87th Congress, 1st Session, 1961.

_____, Committee of the Whole House. Report No.
1299 of July 20, 1955. 84th Congress, 1st
Session, 1955.

_____, Subcommittee No. 1 of the Committee on
Banking and Currency. Hearings on H.R. 6765.
87th Congress, 1st Session, 1961.

U.S. Senate. Report No. 505 of June 10, 1955.
84th Congress, 1st Session, 1955.

_____, Subcommittee of the Committee on Banking
and Currency. Hearings on H.R. 6228. 84th
Congress, 1st Session, 1955.

Books

Boskey, Shirley. Problems and Practices of Develop-
    ment Banks. Baltimore, Md.: The Johns
    Hopkins Press, 1959.

Burns, James M. and Jack W. Peltason. Government
    by the People. Englewood Cliffs, N.J.:
    Prentice-Hall, Inc., 1957.

Friedmann, Wolfgang G., George Kalmanoff, and
    Robert F. Meagher. International Financial
    Aid. New York: Columbia University Press,
    1966.

Hall, Edward T. The Silent Language. New York:
    Doubleday, 1959.

Heilbroner, Robert L. The Great Ascent: The
    Struggle for Economic Development in our Time.
    New York: Harper & Row, 1963.

Hoffmann, Paul G. World Without Want. New York:
    Harper & Row, 1962.

Matecki, B.E. Establishment of the International
    Finance Corporation and United States Policy.
    New York: Frederick A. Praeger, Inc., 1957.

Morris, James. The Road to Huddersfield: A
    Journey to Five Continents. New York:
    Pantheon Books, 1963.

Nyhart, J.D., and Edmond F. Janssens. A Global
    Directory of Development Finance Institutions
    in Developing Countries. Paris: The Devel-
    opment Centre of the Organisation for Economic
    Co-operation and Development, 1967.

Reader's Digest 1967 Almanac and Yearbook.
    Pleasantville, N.Y.: The Reader's Digest
    Association, Inc., 1967.

Riemann, Guenther, and Edwin F. Wigglesworth (eds.).
    The Challenge of International Finance. New
    York: McGraw-Hill, 1966.

Theobald, Robert. The Rich and the Poor: A Study
    of the Economics of Rising Expectations.
    New York: The New American Library of World
    Literature, 1960.

The United Nations & the Business World. New York:
    Business International, 1967.

                Articles and Periodicals

Bennet, William L. "Developing Private Enterprise
        Internationally," Commerce, Vol. 62 (March,
        1965), 9-10.

"Business Pointing Up," The Ross Report of Inves-
        tor's Mexican Letter, XI, No. 8 (April 20,
        1967), 1-3.

Glass, Andrew J. "...and Now to the Bank," The New
        Republic, Vol. 158 (February 17, 1968), 22-23.

Goldberg, Ray A. "Agribusiness for Developing
        Countries," Harvard Business Review, Vol. 44,
        No. 5 (September-October, 1966), 81-93.

Grenier, David. "IFC: An Expanded Role for Ven-
        ture Capital," Finance and Development, IV
        (June, 1967), 133-142.

Halmos, Jr., E.E. "The IFC's engineering depart-
        ment," Worldwide P&I Planning, Vol. 1
        (September/October, 1967), 52-59.

International Financial News Survey, Vol. 19
        (January 13, 1967), 7.

"International Outlook," Business Week, No. 1998
        (December 23, 1967), pp. 62-63.

Laurent, Charles K. and Aquileo Parra A. "Use of
    Mail Questionnaires in Colombia," Journal of
    Marketing Research, V (February, 1968),
    101-103.

Lee, James A. "Cultural Analysis in Overseas
    Operations," Harvard Business Review, XLIV
    (March-April, 1966), 106-114.

Mendels, M.M. "IFC: investment banker to world
    free enterprise," Industrial Canada, June,
    1966, pp. 1-6.

McLean, John G. "Financing Overseas Expansion,"
    Harvard Business Review, XLI (March-April,
    1963), 53-65.

Rockefeller, David. "The Case for Foreign Aid,"
    World Business (May, 1967), pp. 6-7.

Rosen, Martin M. "International Finance Corpora-
    tion: Its Policies and Operations," Euro-
    pean Business Review, September, 1965,
    pp. 1-12.

Wadia, Maneck S. "The Concept of Culture," Journal
    of Retailing, XLI (Spring, 1965), 21-29, 55.

Williams, Simon. "Private Investment in World
    Agriculture," Harvard Business Review,
    43, No. 6 (November-December, 1965), 95-105.

Reports

Annual Report 1966. Lahore, West Pakistan:
    Packages Ltd., 1967.

Annual Report 1965/1966. Mikumi, Tanzania:
    Kilombero Sugar Company Limited, 1966.

Annual Report and Accounts 1966. Bombay: Mahindra
    Ugine Steel Company, Ltd., 1967.

Annual Report Fiscal Year 1965. Monterrey, Mexico:
      Compañia Fundidora de Fierro y Acero de
      Monterrey, S.A., 1965.

Annual Reports of the International Bank for Recon-
      struction and Development. Washington, D.C.:
      IBRD, 1949-1968.

Annual Reports of the International Finance Corpora-
      tion. Washington, D.C.: IFC, 1957-1967.

Annual Report of Ismail Cement Industries Limited
      Ismailwal, West Pakistan, June 30, 1966.

Esto es FEMSA. Madrid, Spain: Fábrica Española
      Magnetos S.A., 1967.

Ford Foundation. A Richer Harvest: A Report on
      Ford Foundation Grants in Overseas Agricul-
      ture. New York: Ford Foundation, 1967.

International Bank for Reconstruction and Develop-
      ment. The Proposed International Finance
      Corporation. Washington, D.C.: IBRD, 1955.

_____. The World Bank Group at Work. Washington,
      D.C.: IBRD, 1967.

_____. The World Bank Group in Africa. Washing-
      ton, D.C.: IBRD, 1963.

_____. The World Bank Group in Brazil. Washing-
      ton, D.C.: IBRD, 1967.

_____. The World Bank Group in Mexico. Washing-
      ton, D.C.: IBRD, 1967.

_____. The World Bank Group in the Americas.
      Washington, D.C.: IBRD, 1963.

_____. The World Bank Group in Tunisia. Washing-
      ton, D.C.: IBRD, 1967.

International Finance Corporation. Accounting and
      Financial Reporting. Washington, D.C.: IFC,
      1964.

_____. Private Development Finance Companies.
    Washington, D.C.:   IFC, 1964.

Memoria y Balance General al 31 de Diciembre de
    1966. Lima, Peru: Fertilizantes Sinteticos
    S.A. (FERTISA)

National Advisory Commission on Food and Fiber.
    The United States Food and Fiber System in a
    Changing World Environment. Washington, D.C.:
    National Advisory Commission on Food and
    Fiber, 1967.

National Advisory Council. The Eighth Special
    Report of the National Advisory Council on
    International Monetary and Financial Prob-
    lems. House Document No. 175, 88th Congress,
    1st Session. Washington, D.C.: U.S. Govern-
    ment Printing Office, 1963.

Report for the Year Ended 31st May 1967. Addis
    Ababa: Cotton Company of Ethiopia, 1967.

The Second Five-year Plan for Development of
    Science and Technology, 1967-1971. Seoul,
    Korea: Government of the Republic of Korea,
    1966.

United Nations, Department of Economic and Social
    Affairs. The United Nations Development
    Decade: Proposals for Action. New York:
    United Nations, 1962.

_____. Economic and Social Council. A Report on
    the Status of the Proposal for an Internation-
    al Finance Corporation. New York, 1953.
    E/2441.

_____. Economic and Social Council. Second
    Report on the Status of the Proposal for an
    International Finance Corporation. New York,
    1954. E/2616.

United States Agency for International Development.
    The Foreign Assistance Program, Annual Report
    to the Congress FY 1966. Washington, D.C.:
    AID, 1968.

_____. The Foreign Assistance Program, Annual
    Report to the Congress FY 1967. Washington,
    D.C.: AID, 1968.

_____. Proposed Foreign Aid Program FY 1968.
    Washington, D.C.: AID, 1967.

World Bank Group. The Role of National Development
    Finance Companies in Industrial Development.
    An Information Paper prepared for the Inter-
    national Symposium on Industrial Development
    sponsored by the United Nations Industrial
    Development Organization, Athens, Greece,
    December, 1967.

Unpublished Material

Friedman, Irving S. "International Problems of
    Economic Development." Address before the
    Canadian Political Science Association,
    Ottawa, Canada, June 7, 1967.

Fundidora de Fierro y Acero de Monterrey, S.A.
    "Cia. Fundidora de Fierro y Acero de Mon-
    terrey, S.A., Mexico." Monterrey, Mexico:
    Fundidora, 1960.

Gaud, William S. "The Green Revolution: Accom-
    plishments and Apprehensions." Address
    before the Tenth World Conference, Society
    for International Development, Washington,
    D.C., March 8, 1968.

Knapp, J. Burke. "The Role of International
    Agencies in Aiding World Food Production."
    Address before the National Academy of
    Science's Scientific Program, Washington,
    D.C., April 25, 1966.

Kuiper, E.T., Douglas Gustafson, and P.M. Mathew.
     "Some Aspects of Policy and Operation of
     Development Finance Companies." Washington,
     D.C.: IFC, 1967. (mimeographed)

Rosen, Martin M. "Financing Fertilizer Production
     in the Developing Countries." Address before
     the First International Agribusiness Confer-
     ence, Chicago, May 10, 1967.

_____. "Industrial Promotion." Address before
     the First International Meeting of Financial
     Institutions for Development, Caracas,
     Venezuela, February 18, 1964.

_____. "IFC and the Growing Need for Private
     Investment in the Low Income Countries."
     Address before the Seminar on International
     Development, York University School of
     Business, Toronto, Canada, November 7, 1967.

_____. "Private Investment in the Developing
     Countries." Address before the National
     Convocation on World Hunger, New York,
     September 12, 1967.

Schmidt, Orvis A. "The World Bank Group in Latin
     America." Address before the Canadian Inter-
     American Association, Montreal, Canada,
     March 2, 1966.

U Thant. "North versus South." Address before the
     Fifth World Conference, Society for Inter-
     national Development, New York, March, 1963.

Woods, George D. "Development--The Need for New
     Directions." Address before the Swedish
     Bankers Association, Stockholm, October 27,
     1967.

Other Sources

Abs, Hermann J., Director, Deutsche Bank. Personal
     letter. February 19, 1968.

Articles of Agreement of the International Finance
     Corporation. Washington, D.C.: IFC, 1956.

Chase Manhattan Bank. Press Release. October 11,
     1961.

Fertilizantes Sinteticos S.A. (FERTISA). Personal
     letter. August 29, 1967.

Foreign Embassies. Personal interviews with various
     officials of Brazilian, Indian, Kenyan,
     Pakistani, and Turkish Embassies. Spring,
     1967.

Hussain, Syed Irshad, Director and General Manager,
     Packages, Ltd. Personal letter. June 10,
     1967.

International Finance Corporation. Personal inter-
     view with Chauncey Dewey, IFC Investment
     Officer. February 16, 1968.

_____. Personal interview with William Diamond,
     Director, IFC Development Finance Companies
     Department. February 14, 1968.

_____. Personal interviews with Donald C. Eynon,
     IFC Investment Officer. October 26, 1967 and
     February 14, 1968.

_____. Personal interview with Ernesto Franco,
     IFC European Investment Officer. February 16,
     1968.

_____. Personal interview with Frank Lamson-
     Scribner, IFC Loan Officer. October 26, 1967.

_____. Personal interview with Peter Muth, IFC
     Investment Officer. February 16, 1968.

_____. Personal interview with Judhvir Parmar,
      IFC Investment Officer. January 18, 1967.

_____. Personal interview with James S. Raj, Vice
      President, IFC. February 23, 1968.

_____. Personal interview with Martin M. Rosen,
      Executive Vice President, IFC. April 17,
      1968.

_____. Press Releases, 1957-1968.

Lobl, A.C., Director, Papel e Celulose, S.A.
      Personal letter. August 22, 1967.

Mistry, P.O., Secretary, Mahindra Ugine Steel
      Company, Ltd. Personal letter. July 13,
      1967.

Summary Proceedings, 1964 Annual Meeting of the
      Board of Governors. Washington, D.C.:   IFC,
      1964.

U.S. Department of State. Personal interview with
      Jay Grahame, Country Desk Officer--India.
      March 23, 1967.

_____. Personal interviews with various officials.
      Spring, 1967.

INDEX

INDEX

ABOUT THE AUTHOR

James C. Baker has been Assistant Professor of
Business Administration at the University of Mary-
land since 1965, and has served as a member of the
Maryland Regional Export Expansion Council and of
the Trade Development Committee of the Baltimore
Chamber of Commerce. In September, 1968, he will
become Associate Professor of World Business at the
Center for World Business, San Francisco State
College.

Dr. Baker received his doctorate in international business administration from Indiana University. He is the co-editor (with John K. Ryans, Jr.)
of World Marketing: A Multinational Approach, published in 1967 by John Wiley & Sons. In addition,
he has written extensively on the German securities
exchanges and has had articles published in Michi-
gan State University Business Topics, German American Trade News, University of Washington Business
Review, Temple University Bulletin of Business and
Economics, and Marquette University Business Review.